Editor

Erica N. Russikoff, M.A.

Editor in Chief

Karen J. Goldfluss, M.S. Ed.

Creative Director

Sarah M. Fournier

Cover Artist

Barb Lorseyedi

Imaging

Amanda R. Harter

Publisher

Mary D. Smith, M.S. Ed.

Authors

Peter and Sheryl Sloan

For correlations to the Common Core State Standards, see pages 78–80 of this book or visit *http://www.teachercreated.com/standards/*.

Teacher Created Resources

12621 Western Avenue

Garden Grove, CA 92841

www.teachercreated.com

ISBN: 978-1-4206-8381-3

©2016 Teacher Created Resources

Made in U.S.A.

Teacher Created Resources

Table of Contents

Introduction

Literacy Power was developed as a tool for teachers who are looking to support or enhance an existing reading and language-arts curriculum. The *Literacy Power* series provides teachers and students with an alternative approach to grade-appropriate material and allows teachers to reinforce reading, writing, and language skills with their students through diverse and engaging units.

Each *Literacy Power* book includes a variety of text types, such as narrative, procedural, and recount, as well as an assortment of comprehension activities inspired by the text. Each book contains a variety of high-interest topics that aim at addressing reading and writing skills in an in-depth way.

The activities in this series promote higher-level thinking and can be used to teach specific skills, reinforce information previously taught, or simply provide additional practice.

Sample activities across the series include the following:

- reading for information
- following procedures
- responding to writing prompts
- understanding details
- combining sentences
- using words in context
- determining fact or fiction
- sequencing
- interpreting pictures
- comparing and contrasting
- organizing information
- defining new vocabulary
- drawing conclusions
- matching

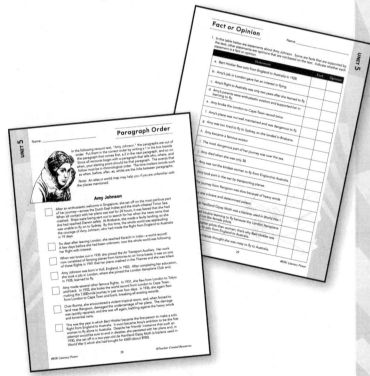

Standards

The Common Core is a set of highly researched academic standards created by teachers, school chiefs, administrators, and other educational experts. The goal of the standards is for students required to graduate high school with the same skill set and academic knowledge to succeed in future endeavors. In order for this to occur, a set of common objectives needs to be met for each grade level.

To help students become career ready, all of the texts and activities in the *Literacy Power* series have been aligned to the Common Core State Standards. To learn more about these standards, visit *http://www.corestandards.org/* or *http://www.teachercreated.com/standards/*.

How to Use This Book

The book is divided into separate units, each with a particular theme structure—either content themes or process themes. These themes are interwoven both conceptually and structurally. The content themes are based on the interests of students at their particular age and grade levels. The process themes focus on reading and writing processes.

Literacy Power provides students with a variety of opportunities to review classroom content. The activities can be used as independent or small-group practice, or they can provide teachers with opportunities for in-depth, whole-class instruction. Regardless of how you choose to use this book, the following tips may be helpful in implementing the program in your classroom.

- Introduce the workbook to your students and explain that the activities in the book will provide them with the opportunity to think about and interact with some of the concepts being taught in class, but possibly from a slightly different approach.

- Explain that the pages are designed to be easily understood. The instructions for each activity are concise and were written to be as clear as possible. Remind students to read the directions for every activity very carefully, as each activity typically requires something slightly different. Depending on the level of your students, you may want to first read the directions as a group and answer any questions.

- Allow students time to flip through the workbook to become more familiar with the layout of the pages and the various activities. Discuss any themes or activities that they seem particularly excited about or pages that pique their interest.

- Give students ample time to complete each activity, and then discuss as a class afterwards. Make note of any activities or concepts that may be more difficult and may require further review or additional instruction.

- On occasion, allow students to complete activity pages with partners. Having a discussion about the content and questions is a great way to build fluency, collaboration skills, and shared knowledge.

- *Literacy Power* was developed to focus on skills and content appropriate for a particular grade level. If you find some of your students are struggling with the content or completing the activities too quickly, consider locating a similar activity from one of the other books in the *Literacy Power* series intended for either a younger or older grade level.

Before reading the text, think about this question:

> ### Who, besides Aboriginal Australians, were the "discoverers" of Australia?

1. Write your answer here. *(Do not read the text.)*

   _____

   _____

   _____

2. Share your answer with your group and discuss everyone's answers. Write your group's answer here.

   _____

   _____

   _____

3. Now read the text below, keeping in mind the question you have just discussed.

> This activity is best done in a group or with a partner. This unit uses activities to guide you as you read and discuss what you read.
>
> 1. Follow the activity step by step.
>
> 2. Only do what the activity asks.
>
> 3. Be sure to have a dictionary handy in case you need to get the definition of a word in the text.
>
> 4. Since you are working in a group, you must be prepared to allow everyone to finish a task before progressing to the next.

Who Discovered Australia?

1. Ask the question, "Who discovered Australia?" and any Australian is likely to say that the Dutch traders and explorers of the 17th century were the first to land on the coast, followed by seafarers, such as Abel Tasman and, in time, James Cook. Wrong! Well, wrong if you believe what seems to be an enormous amount of evidence to show that, far from being unknown to the rest of the world until recent times, Australia was visited and settled by many different peoples for thousands of years.

2. Australia sits between two great oceans: the Indian and the Pacific. It is in the path of trading routes that have been sailed for thousands of years. The Great South Land, or Island, was, so some people believe, known to the ancient civilizations of Egypt, India, Sumeria, Phoenicia, Greece, Rome, China, and Japan. Some say that it was even known to the Vikings. Not only do they say the land was known to these peoples, but also that they journeyed here and mined gold and other metals.

3. Aboriginal Australian legends and paintings appear to show that other peoples besides themselves have visited Australia. Some examples of other "evidence" that apparently show Australia was visited in early times are given in the reports that follow.

4. One day in 1931 at Glenloth, Victoria, on the shore of what was once a lake, 10-year-old John Gibbs was playing in the sand and shell remains of an ancient Aboriginal campsite. In the sandhills among the broken shells, he picked up a large lump of petrified mud. Sticking out from one of the mud pieces was a small bronze coin.

5. Years later, a Melbourne Museum coin expert identified it as a Greek coin that had been made in Egypt over 2,200 years ago. One explanation for where it was found is that it perhaps had been left behind by ancient visitors—Greek explorers, or even Arabs, Indians, or Malayans— with whom the Greeks traded.

Who Discovered Australia? *(cont.)*

6. In 1961, a family picnicking on the Daly River, in the Northern Territory, found a gold scarab (beetle), an object of worship to the ancient Egyptians. How did this valuable piece of jewelry come to be found in such a remote location?

7. Another example is a 2,000-year-old carved stone head of the ancient Chinese goddess, Shao Lin, the protector of sailors, which was discovered on a hillside on the far south coast of New South Wales.

8. There are supposedly many ancient rock inscriptions in Phoenician, Libyan, Egyptian, Celtic, Scandinavian, and other languages that have been found across Australia. People are said to have found many interesting relics and megalithic ruins, left here by seafaring adventurers who came from civilizations now long extinct. They used the world's oceans as marine "highways" as they sailed in search of new lands rich in gold, silver, copper, tin, gemstones, and pearls.

9. The theory is that some of the peoples not only discovered and mined the mysterious "Great Southern Land" and its island neighbors, but also established colonies that were large enough to require villages and towns. By the time they vanished, these ancient settlers had left behind large ruins and temples, tombs and pyramids, and rock writing in a great number of ancient tongues. These relics are said to puzzle historians because they show that ancient peoples had the ability to construct and navigate large boats. People, apparently, were traveling hundreds of years before the invention of a written language, and the watercraft they sailed in was big, strong, and seaworthy.

10. Australia, so the story goes, had always been known to someone. Most likely, sailors from southeast Asia were the first to find it. They passed on the story of their discovery to the Indo-Aryans of the Indus Valley, to the Sumerians and, in time, to the Babylonians and Persians and others, such as the Celts and even Vikings. The Greeks and, later, the Romans, followed, and the Indian and Pacific oceans became oceanic highways. In time, these seaways provided easier—and safer—trade routes to and from lands that once could only be reached by hard, dangerous land travel.

11. At the same time, the great civilizations on the opposite side of the Pacific, in the Americas, were also going to sea in sailing vessels, taking large numbers of people, with food and animals, across the central Pacific. Those who returned told stories of the fabulous lands over the waters past the western horizon.

12. Australia sits between two oceans that make up two great marine highways by which the people of the ancient world could come to exploit the continent's riches. There are maps showing Australia, which are claimed to have been drawn long before its discovery by explorers in modern times.

13. The Greek philosopher, Anaximander, is said to have drawn a world map in Myletus, describing a southern continent. Theopompus of Chios, in the 4th century B.C.E., supposedly drew a similar world map and wrote that, "a great island lay beyond India"—in the region where Australia is situated. In 239 B.C.E., Eratosthenes, the Greek scholar, allegedly drew a world map as a globe, on which he described a great southern continent. Around 150 B.C.E., Crates of Mallos constructed a 10-foot diameter world globe, upon which he depicted four continents divided by two great oceans. These seem to indicate that maritime and geographical knowledge was far more advanced in the ancient world than was realized by many historians.

Who Discovered Australia? *(cont.)*

14. People who live on the islands to the north of Australia have some religious and family customs that seem to be related to ancient Egypt. In 1975, at Gympie in Queensland, an Egyptian-type "pyramid" about 100 feet high, as well as other Egyptian artifacts, were allegedly discovered. These were said to be at least 6,000 years old. The "pyramid" is on the shore of what was once a harbor. Aboriginal legends are said to tell about these ancient explorers who visited in large bird-like canoes and built the pyramid. According to some people, they also dug holes in the ground and took away rocks from this ancient mining area.

15. In 1994, many stones were found at rich gemstone locations in Queensland and New South Wales. They are claimed to have Egyptian, Phoenician, and Canaanite writing on them.

16. Australia is said to have been visited by the Chinese, using detailed maps of Australia dating from about 600 B.C.E. to 800 C.E. Their records, so it is claimed, describe Australia as being the home of a race of small black people. Their writings supposedly even describe kangaroos and other Australian animals. If these writings are true, it would seem the east coast of Australia was explored frequently by Chinese traders and explorers.

17. Some Japanese history books allegedly record that, in the early 15th century, their sailors voyaged to Australia in search of pearls. The famous Japanese warrior explorer, Yamada Nagamasa, with a fleet of 40 ships, is claimed to have explored every land from Japan to Australia, between 1620 and 1633. Japanese texts of that time apparently refer to Australia as *Sei-yo*, which is supposed to mean, "The great southern land," and *Sei-tso*, or "The south land of pearls." Some people believe Japanese contact dates back at least 2,000 years.

18. If any evidence briefly stated here is correct, it shows that for many thousands of years, Australia was visited by sailors from other countries, who came in search of gold and silver and other metals and gems.

19. Australia may well be the oldest place inhabited by humans on Earth. Remains of large, stone structures said to have been found in Australia and in other parts of the Pacific are supposedly 10,000 to 20,000 years old.

20. So, who discovered Australia? Take your pick from the many ancient and not-so ancient civilizations that came there. We may never know who was the first, but we do know that it was a long time ago and that Australia was never "the lost continent."

Answering Questions

1. Now that you have read the text "Who Discovered Australia?" who, besides the Aboriginals, do you think may have been the discoverers of Australia?

   _____

   _____

   _____

   _____

Name: _____

Answering Questions *(cont.)*

2. Discuss how your answer to question #2 on page 5 compares to your answer now that you have read the text. After your group discussion, write your group's revised answer to the question.

_____

_____

_____

_____

_____

_____

Completing a Meaning Grid

1. Indicate whether each statement below is true, false, or there is no evidence to decide either way, by writing the paragraph number in the correct box. Compare your answers and share your reasons with your group.

Statement	True	False	No Evidence
a. The ancient Sumerians were the first group to come to Australia.			
b. No one had ever visited Australia before the Aboriginal Australians.			
c. Ocean travel over long distances was easier than land travel.			
d. Most seafarers came to Australia for timber.			
e. Remains of towns and villages show that some groups of adventurers stayed for a long time.			
f. No one knew that Earth was round before Columbus sailed to America in 1492.			
g. Chinese maps were very lacking in detail.			
h. Historians have had to question their ideas about Australia's discovery.			
i. The Australian land was extremely harsh, which explains why none of the visitors remained there.			
j. Aboriginal Australians had contact with some of the ancient visitors to their shores.			

Providing Proof

Find and write the examples from the "Who Discovered Australia?" text that show each of the statements below is true. Complete your answers before discussing them with your group.

1. Give at least two examples that prove the Chinese visited Australia long before European discoveries.

   a. _____

   _____

   b. _____

   _____

2. Give at least two examples that prove that ancient Egyptians came to Australia.

   a. _____

   _____

   b. _____

   _____

3. Ancient visitors came to Australia to get (a) gold, (b) precious stones, and (c) pearls. Give three examples to prove this.

   a. _____

   _____

   b. _____

   _____

   c. _____

   _____

4. The location of Australia between two great oceans was very important for ancient traders. Give an example to prove this.

   _____

   _____

   _____

   _____

5. There is evidence that some visitors stayed a long time in Australia. Give an example to prove this.

   _____

   _____

   _____

   _____

Name: _____

Words in Context

1. In the table below are words or definitions that mean the same as words in the text. Find the word in the text and write it in the box. The paragraph where the word is found is given as a clue.

Word/Definition	Paragraph	Text Word/Group of Words
a. very large amount	1	
b. advanced cultures	2	
c. groups of people living together	9	
d. the original settlers	3	
e. veneration	6	
f. very risky	10	
g. objects from the past	9	
h. rubies and opals	18	
i. understood	13	
j. ships	11	
k. lived in	19	
l. languages	9	
m. good at floating	9	
n. hardened like rock	4	
o. large, tapered stone building	14	

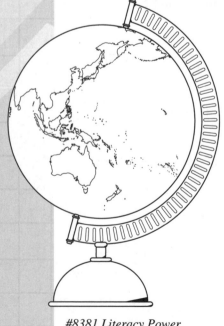

Matching

1. Match the person/object on the left with the place on the right.

   a. John Gibbs   • Japan

   b. Theopompus   • Mallos

   c. Egyptian "pyramid"   • Myletus

   d. Yamada Nagamasa   • China

   e. Anaximander   • Chios

   f. Family of picnickers   • Gympie

   g. Shao Lin   • Daly River

   h. Crates   • Victoria

Combining Sentences

Name: _____

1. Below are groups of sentences. Write one sentence that has the same meaning as the sentences in each group. One has been done for you.

a. Most people think this.
   Australia was discovered by Dutch traders.
   The truth is this.
   Australia was probably visited by many ancient civilizations thousands of years ago.

   Most people think that Australia was discovered by Dutch traders, but the truth
   is that Australia was probably visited by many ancient civilizations thousands of
   years ago.

b. Australia lies between oceans.
   The oceans are the Indian and the Pacific.
   It is on the trade routes between these two oceans.
   These trade routes have been sailed for thousands of years.

   _____
   _____
   _____

c. There is a lot of evidence.
   The evidence shows that Australia was visited.
   It was visited by Ancient Egyptians, Chinese, Greeks, and others.
   The visiting took place over thousands of years.

   _____
   _____
   _____

d. There are many ancient world maps.
   The maps are over 2,000 years old.
   The maps show a large land.
   The land is where Australia is.

   _____
   _____
   _____

e. There can be no doubt.
   Australia was known.
   It was known for thousands of years.
   This is long before the Dutch traders.

   _____
   _____
   _____

UNIT 2

Name: _____

Writing a Letter

1. Read the imaginary letter below.

> Cave 3149
> Volcano Road
> Rock City, Mars
> 45th of Disgust 10245
>
> Dear Earthling,
>
> Greetings from Mars. My name is Bam Hurger. I am a Martian boy who is only 250 years old. I have a younger sister called Trench Tries who is just a baby—100 years old.
>
> At school I am in Grade 91. That means I have been in Grade 1 for 90 years. My favorite subjects are volcano sliding and lava cooking.
>
> I am going to town soon to get a hot, sulfur-flavored lava drink and a rock lizard burger from Lavaland.
>
> Yours sincerely,
> Bam Hurger

2. In the space below, write an imaginary letter from an alien to a friend on Earth. Use the example above to guide you. Change some of the things in the example and add your own information.

   Write a draft of your letter below and then proofread it. Write your final copy on the next page.

_____

_____

_____

_____

_____

_____

_____

_____

_____

_____

_____

_____

_____

Writing a Letter *(cont.)*

Name: _____

3. Read #2 on page 12. Write the final copy of your letter below.

_____

_____

_____

_____

_____

_____

_____

_____

_____

_____

_____

_____

_____

_____

_____

_____

_____

_____

_____

_____

_____

_____

_____

Letter-Writing Format

The box contains an example of a personal letter. A letter has five parts, each of which is separated by a blank line.

The **sender's address** and **date**	*12 Wood Street* *Salt Lake City, UT 84108* *February 1, 2016*
The **greeting**	*Dear Mr. Jones,*
The **body** of the letter (full punctuation as in normal writing)	*Thank you for feeding my dog while we were away on vacation. I hope that Scruffy was well behaved for you.*
End remarks (the closing)	*Yours sincerely,*
Space for signature	
Name	*Emma Plod*

Emails follow the same system, except that the computer puts in the sender's email address for replies.

Any type of text may comprise the body of the letter. If, for example, the body of the text is a recount (such as a letter telling about a person's travels to another place), then the body of the letter will have the structure of a recount with a setting, events, and an ending.

In the days before telephones and, more recently, computers, letter writing was practiced a great deal. It is still widely used today, especially in business affairs where a written record is required or when the same message has to be sent to many different people.

1. Which of the following situations is suited to the use of a letter as a means of communication? Check *yes* or *no* to indicate suitability. Give a short reason for your answer.

   a. Sending an important invitation that requires a reply | yes | | no |

   Reason: _____

   _____

   _____

b. A lawyer sending an important document to be signed   [yes]   [no]

Reason: _____

_____

_____

c. Applying for a job   [yes]   [no]

Reason: _____

_____

_____

d. Asking your mother, who lives in the same house, where your shirt is   [yes]   [no]

Reason: _____

_____

_____

e. Filing a complaint about damaged goods   [yes]   [no]

Reason: _____

_____

_____

f. Communicating with a friend whose telephone is not connected   [yes]   [no]

Reason: _____

_____

_____

g. Giving instructions to a friend on how to set up a computer   [yes]   [no]

Reason: _____

_____

_____

h. Ordering a taxi to pick you up today   [yes]   [no]

Reason: _____

_____

_____

i. Giving permission to a friend to use your bicycle   [yes]   [no]

Reason: _____

_____

_____

Name: _____

Interpreting Information

As you read, think about this question:

> **Why is paragliding becoming so popular?**

You may wish to highlight some parts of the text that can help you answer this.

The Sport of Paragliding

Paragliding started in the mid-1900s. This sport allows people to soar and glide with the same ease as birds. It has attracted a huge following in a short time. It is claimed to be the world's most popular aerial sport, on the basis of the number of **participants**.

In **aviation** terms, it is also said to have attracted the highest number of female pilots of any flying activity. Thousands of men and women have already become qualified paraglider pilots.

So what are the advantages of paragliding over other **aerial** activities?

1. It's easy to learn. Rather than the months it takes to gain a fixed-wing license, learning to paraglide takes just a few days.

2. The equipment is easy to operate. A paraglider is, by design, a **stable** platform. It is easy to steer. No special or advanced skills are needed to fly and **maneuver**. Take-offs happen at low speeds and, if necessary, can easily be **aborted**. Even landing is easy—you land on your own two feet rather than wheels! (Some paragliders have wheels, but that's another story!)

3. It's quick to set up and pack up. Time is always important when it's limited—but even someone with very little time would have to agree that one minute to set up and under five minutes to pack up is pretty speedy.

4. You don't need any special **physical** skills or training. Forget about complicated physical tasks! If you are old enough (over 15) and don't have any **disabling** conditions or illnesses, you'll be able to paraglide.

5. It doesn't cost a lot to start paragliding. Anything to do with aviation is expensive, but paragliding is relatively cheap, both for training and equipment.

6. You can fly almost anywhere. No need for airports or landing strips; paragliders can launch from almost any place—fields, roads, beaches, even parks (where allowed). And there's no need to worry about fuel either. Once you're in the air, you can use **thermals** and **topography** to stay up there for hours. If you're good enough, you can even fly hundreds of miles cross-country.

7. It's a safe sport. In fact, of all the aerial sports, paragliding is reputed to be one of the safest. Why? Well, the equipment is easy to use, it's built to strict guidelines, and it's been proven over many years. Even if something does go terribly wrong, paragliders are equipped with . . . you guessed it . . . a **reserve** parachute!

The Sport of Paragliding (cont.)

How Do You Learn To Fly?

You learn to fly in stages. Students start off with basic training and progress to more advanced training as their skill levels increase. The training course may be something like the following.

Basic Training

As the name says, this covers the basic aspects, both in theory (about two hours) and in practice (between 10 and 15 hours, approximately).

In the practical part, students learn safety skills and procedures, inflation of the paraglider, and take-offs and landings. Take-offs are usually from a sand dune at a beach, or somewhere similar.

In fact, a broad beach is a good place to learn, because there is generally a constant **breeze** and soft sand to launch from and land on. Naturally, the beach mustn't be too narrow—no one wants to land in the water.

High-Altitude Training

This extends the skills learned in basic training, and flights are generally longer. A **minimum** of 12 flights is required, and these are spread across four or five training sessions. Because of the high-**altitude** component, **alternative** sites are often used to launch, some of them several hundred feet high.

These flights generally use a more advanced paraglider, and the student carries a two-way radio and wears a harness with back protection and a spare parachute.

Most training schools will use two instructors—one for take-off and another for landing. Once the student passes the course, he or she receives a level 1 license. This can be extended by further training, including staying in the air for three or even four hours at a time.

Advanced Training

There is a theoretical and a practical component to this training as well. About half a day is required for the theory lessons, with time also spent on improving take-off technique. The students will also learn and practice thermal flying, that is, using rising currents of air to be carried upwards. Cross-country flying is often included as well.

One exciting area covered during advanced training is cable-assisted take-offs, where a power winch and cable are used to launch the paraglider, not unlike the way you run to launch a kite. The students generally need to make six successful cable-assisted take-offs to pass this section of the course.

Summary

Paragliding is an addictive sport; people who participate say that, for thrills and enjoyment, there is nothing else like it. Compared with most other high-action sports, paragliding is cheap and safe but very exciting.

Name: _____

Words in Context

Words have meaning in context. This means that a word's meaning depends on the theme or the subject of the text. For example, the word "bear" means a different thing in each of these sentences.

*The load was more than he could **bear**.*
*The man was careful as he knew a **bear** was nearby.*

1. Using a dictionary, write the definition that best fits each word below in the context of paragliding. (These words are boldfaced in the text.)

   a. aviation _____
   _____

   b. participants _____
   _____

   c. altitude _____
   _____

   d. aborted _____
   _____

   e. stable _____
   _____

   f. maneuver _____
   _____

   g. physical _____
   _____

   h. disabling _____
   _____

   i. thermals _____
   _____

   j. topography _____
   _____

   k. aerial _____
   _____

   l. reserve _____
   _____

Words in Context *(cont.)*

Name: _____

m. breeze _____

_____

n. minimum _____

_____

o. alternative _____

_____

Supporting an Answer

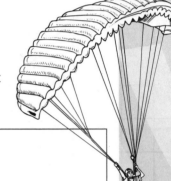

1. Answer the guiding question: **Why is paragliding becoming so popular?**
   Here are some reasons. You can add more of your own on a separate sheet
   of paper if you wish. Now you must explain why these reasons would make
   paragliding popular. One has been done for you.

Reasons Paragliding Is Becoming Popular

- *Paragliding is easy to learn.*

  *If a sport is easy to learn, more people are able to take it up and gain enjoyment.
  If it is hard to learn, many people would not be interested, as it would be too long
  before they could glide.*

- **It is easy to do.**

  _____

  _____

  _____

  _____

- **It is fairly cheap.**

  _____

  _____

  _____

  _____

- **It doesn't take a lot of time to get started and to finish.**

  _____

  _____

  _____

Name: _____

Reasons Paragliding Is Becoming Popular (cont.)

- *Paragliding is not physically difficult.*

_____

_____

_____

_____

_____

- *It is a very safe aerial sport.*

_____

_____

_____

_____

_____

- *You can paraglide from many different places.*

_____

_____

_____

_____

_____

- *It is open to all ages above 15 and to both men and women.*

_____

_____

_____

_____

_____

Essay Writing

Think of another popular sport. Describe the sport. Explain why people enjoy participating in it. Do you like it? Tell why or why not.

_____

_____

_____

_____

_____

_____

_____

_____

_____

_____

_____

_____

_____

_____

_____

_____

_____

_____

_____

_____

_____

_____

_____

_____

_____

_____

_____

Name: _____

Library Organization

Read the text below to find out how and why nonfiction books are organized in libraries.

The Dewey Decimal System

Libraries do not put their books just anywhere on the shelves because it would be hard to remember where a book is. In addition, users would have no idea where to look. Sometimes, a user does not know what books there are on a topic and just wants a brief look at what is available. Having all the books on the same topic in the same place helps readers find what they want. Once, books in libraries were sorted by size, and that meant books on a given topic were scattered everywhere within the shelves.

Today, books in libraries are sorted very carefully so that, no matter where the library is, it will be organized the same way as other libraries in the world. The system for doing this is called the Dewey Decimal System, which was invented by Melvil Dewey. In this system, books are given a number according to their subject and filed in topic categories. The table below shows the main categories of the Dewey system.

Decimal Classification	Topic Category
0–099	General Works, Encyclopedias, Journals
100–199	Philosophy and Psychology
200–299	Religion and Mythology
300–399	Social Sciences
400–499	Languages
500–599	Natural Science (mathematics, physics, chemistry, astronomy, geology, etc.)
600–699	Technology (engineering, agriculture, home economics, computers, etc.)
700–799	The Arts (music, architecture, sports, etc.)
800–899	Literature
900–999	History, Geography, Travel, Biographies

When readers know what topics interest them, they can go directly to that classification. If the readers examine the library catalog for a book, they can use the name of the book and its decimal number to find it. Each book has its own classification number and a decimal number that shows where it is located within that group. For example, the book *Astronomy Today* (504.325) can be found in the Natural Science category (504), and its location is 325 in that section.

Using the Dewey System

Name: _____

1. Write the Dewey category to show where you would find a book on each of the topics below.

Topic	Dewey Category	Topic	Dewey Category
a. Dictionaries		i. Learning French	
b. How to be a better athlete		j. Presidents of the U.S.A.	
c. Germany		k. Animals	
d. Marine biology		l. Safety in the home	
e. Galaxies		m. Ancient Egypt	
f. The poems of Edward Lear		n. God, man, and the universe	
g. Mountaineering		o. Cooking Japanese food	
h. Indian elephants		p. History of flight	

Locating Books

1. Write the Dewey decimal classification to show where you would find each of the titles below.

Title	Decimal Classification	Title	Decimal Classification
a. *Fixing the Basic Computer*		i. *Traveling by Train Through India*	
b. *Exploring the Planets*		j. *Practical House Plants*	
c. *The Religions of Man*		k. *The Life of Einstein*	
d. *Great Ideas About Life*		l. *How to Play Guitar*	
e. *Education in Texas*		m. *Karate for Self-defense*	
f. *Children's Encyclopedia*		n. *Cooking Simple Meals*	
g. *Mount Everest*		o. *The Solar System*	
h. *Training Dogs*		p. *How to Speak Spanish*	

Name: _____

Using Proofreading Skills

1. In this activity, the rules concerning the following need to be known: capitalization and punctuation.

   Correct the text by circling where a mistake has been made or something has been left out. Write the corrections above each mistake you find.

Going to the Library on Saturday

one wet saturday my friends and i were bored so we went to the library

to find a book called aliens from the planet chardon written by susan

dull and bob boring the library is located on jones street in ocean view

city susan dull and bob boring live in forest hotel by the banks of the

swift river. bob boring was once a writer for the p.t.a. and then wrote

for the new city times newspaper.

susan dull also wrote scientific articles for animal magazines on the

cougar or as it is scientifically called felis concolor this animal is

becoming rare but the lion preservation society is raising a million

dollars to help preserve them in places such as north carolina

we came home from the library in mr browns car as it was raining

heavily and the girls coats were not enough to keep out the rain

Extending Concepts

Name: _____

1. Circle what each object always has.

Object	Always has . . .			
a. A library	computers	books	DVDs	CDs
b. A book	pictures	chapters	stories	pages
c. A school	playgrounds	libraries	students	computers
d. A dictionary	pictures	idioms	words	sentences
e. An encyclopedia	Internet sites	pictures	essays	information
f. A bookcase	book dividers	books	shelves	labels
g. The Internet	icons	graphics	websites	inboxes
h. A library catalog	a list	books	photographs	stories
i. A bow	arrows	a string	a handgrip	a quiver
j. A jet plane	an engine	passengers	flight attendants	a pilot
k. A kitchen	knives	shelves	a pantry	a sink
l. A flower	petals	a stem	thorns	a smell
m. A bicycle	a bell	pedals	a basket	wheels
n. A fire engine	a hose	a ladder	a water tank	an ax
o. A cat	fur	kittens	a basket	fleas
p. A horse	legs	horseshoes	a long tail	saddles
q. A town	libraries	streets	bridges	schools
r. A TV	legs	wood	a screen	an engine

Name: _____

Classifying Analogies

Some analogies are based on how things can be grouped, or how they can be classified. Fill in the blanks and choose the answer that best completes each analogy.

1. How are carrots and potatoes alike? They are both kinds of _v_____.

2. How are tables and chairs alike? They are both kinds of _f_____.

Hint: Pay attention to order: **carrot : vegetable** is not the same as **vegetable : carrot**!

A *carrot* is always a *vegetable*, but a *vegetable* is not always a *carrot*. So, **table : furniture** is not the same as **furniture : table**.

3. A _t_____ is always a piece of _____.

   A piece of _____ is not always a _____.

---

4. **Everest : mountain**
   a. Nile : Amazon
   b. Amazon : Nile
   c. Nile : river
   d. river : Nile

5. **color : scarlet**
   a. rose : flower
   b. flower : rose
   c. white : daisy
   d. daisy : white

6. **pepper : spice**
   a. quartz : mineral
   b. mineral : quartz
   c. salt : cinnamon
   d. cinnamon : salt

7. **Juneau : capital**
   a. Paris : London
   b. London : Paris
   c. country : Mexico
   d. Mexico : country

8. **organ : heart**
   a. leg : limb
   b. limb : leg
   c. finger : hand
   d. hand : finger

9. **sandal : shoe**
   a. boot : sneaker
   b. sneaker : boot
   c. iron : metal
   d. metal : iron

10. **punctuation : comma**
    a. appliance : stove
    b. stove : appliance
    c. cool : refrigerator
    d. refrigerator : cool

11. **apple : fruit**
    a. orange : banana
    b. banana : orange
    c. grain : wheat
    d. wheat : grain

12. **weapon : cannon**
    a. panther : cat
    b. cat : panther
    c. lion : leopard
    d. leopard : lion

Fill in the blanks and choose the answer that best completes each analogy.

13. How are a poodle and a Saint Bernard alike? They are both _d_____.

14. Why are these word pairs different? **poodle : dog   dog : poodle**

   - A _p_____ is always a _____.
   - A _d_____ is not always a _____.

---

15. **screwdriver : tool**
   - a. boat : canoe
   - b. kayak : boat
   - c. carrot : fruit
   - d. fruit : pear

16. **desert : Sahara**
   - a. cactus : plant
   - b. sedimentary : rock
   - c. ocean : Pacific
   - d. Ganges : river

17. **mouse : rodent**
   - a. salmon : fish
   - b. feline : cheetah
   - c. bird : vulture
   - d. canine : collie

18. **violin : instrument**
   - a. amphibian : frog
   - b. mammal : giraffe
   - c. insect : locust
   - d. crocodile : reptile

19. **Mercury : planet**
   - a. candy : lollipop
   - b. star : Sun
   - c. clothes : shirt
   - d. hip hop : music

20. **haiku : poem**
   - a. flower : tulip
   - b. book : novel
   - c. redwood : tree
   - d. cheese : cheddar

21. **game : basketball**
   - a. Russia : continent
   - b. island : Madagascar
   - c. Africa : country
   - d. ocean : Caribbean

22. **van : vehicle**
   - a. femur : bone
   - b. color : crimson
   - c. dog : poodle
   - d. falls : Niagara

23. **month : October**
   - a. Friday : day
   - b. season : spring
   - c. year : century
   - d. week : seven

Name: _____

Paragraph Order

In the following recount text, "Amy Johnson," the paragraphs are out of order. Put them in the correct order by writing a 1 in the box beside the paragraph that comes first, a 2 in the next paragraph, and so on. Since all recounts begin with a paragraph that tells who, where, and when, your starting point should be that paragraph. The events that follow must be in chronological order. The time markers (words such as *when*, *before*, *after*, *as*, *while*) are the links between paragraphs.

Note: An atlas or world map may help you if you are unfamiliar with the places mentioned.

Amy Johnson

☐ After an enthusiastic welcome in Singapore, she set off on the most perilous part of her journey—across the Dutch East Indies and the shark-infested Timor Sea. When all contact with her plane was lost for 24 hours, it was feared that she had crashed. Ships were being sent out to search for her when the news came that she had reached Darwin safely. At Brisbane, she made a faulty landing, so she was unable to fly on to Sydney. By this time, the whole world was applauding the courage of Amy Johnson, who had made the flight from England to Australia in 19 days.

☐ Six days after leaving London, she reached Karachi in India—a world record! A few days before she had been unknown; now the whole world was following her flight with interest.

☐ When war broke out in 1939, she joined the Air Transport Auxiliary. Her work now consisted of ferrying planes from factories to air force bases; it was on one of these flights in 1941 that her plane crashed in the Thames and she was killed.

☐ Amy Johnson was born in Hull, England, in 1903. After completing her education, she took a job in London, where she joined the London Aeroplane Club and, in 1928, learned to fly.

☐ Amy made several other famous flights. In 1931, she flew from London to Tokyo and back. In 1932, she broke the world record from London to Cape Town, making the 7,000-mile journey in just over four days. In 1936, she again flew from London to Cape Town and back, breaking all existing records.

☐ Over Burma, she encountered a violent tropical storm, and, when forced to land near Rangoon, damaged the undercarriage of her plane. The damage was quickly repaired, and she was off again, battling against the heavy winds and torrential rains.

☐ This was the year in which Bert Hinkler became the first person to make a solo flight from England to Australia. It soon became Amy's ambition to be the first woman to fly alone to Australia. Despite her friends' insistence that such an attempt would be sure to end in disaster, she persisted with her plans and, in 1930, she set off in a two-year-old de Havilland Gipsy Moth (a biplane used in World War I) which she had bought for £600 (about $950).

Fact or Opinion

Name: _____

1. In the table below are statements about Amy Johnson. Some are facts that are supported by the text; other statements are opinions that are not based on the text. Indicate whether each statement is a fact or opinion.

Statement	Fact	Opinion
a. Bert Hinkler flew solo from England to Australia in 1928.		
b. Amy's job in London gave her an interest in flying.		
c. Amy's flight to Australia was only two years after she learned to fly.		
d. Amy's parents were enthusiastic aviators and supported her in learning to fly.		
e. Amy broke the London-to-Cape-Town record twice.		
f. Amy's plane was not well maintained and was dangerous to fly.		
g. Amy was too tired to fly to Sydney, so she landed in Brisbane.		
h. Amy became a famous aviator.		
i. The most dangerous part of her journey was over the sea.		
j. Amy died when she was only 38.		
k. Amy was not the kindest woman to fly from England to Australia.		
l. Amy took part in the war by transporting planes.		
m. The journey from Rangoon was slow because of heavy winds.		
n. Amy was a brave and determined person.		
o. The de Havilland Gipsy Moth was a biplane used in World War I.		
p. Amy had trouble learning to fly because the London Aeroplane Club did not like female pilots.		
q. Men are better pilots than women; that's why Bert Hinkler was the first to fly solo from England to Australia.		
r. All of Amy's friends thought she was crazy to fly to Australia.		

Name: _____

Reading Critically

1. Work in a group of five or six.

2. Read the short story "Marooned" carefully, by yourself.

3. Rank the items in the table in order of importance.

4. When all members of your group have completed their rankings, discuss your answers. Choose group answers for each of the items.

Marooned

You are traveling by plane over the ocean when a sudden storm catches the aircraft. All communication with the outside world is lost as the plane is blown off course in an unknown direction for two hours. Based on the information you have, you are 900 miles from the nearest land mass.

The pilot manages to land the damaged plane on the water, but it begins to sink. The 20 passengers and five crew members are able to get into a large life raft. As the plane sinks, the crew is able to salvage the items below. Since you will not be able to carry them all, rank the items in order of importance for your survival, with 1 being the most important and 15 being the least important.

1.

Item	Your Rank	Group Rank
a. a video camera		
b. a map of the Pacific		
c. 4 blankets		
d. a small mirror		
e. a large piece of canvas		
f. 10 two-liter bottles of water		
g. a roll of mosquito netting		
h. a large torch with good batteries		
i. a computer with a wireless modem		
j. a fishing rod and 10 hooks		
k. a pocketknife		
l. 3 chocolate bars		
m. 6 large cans of soup		
n. 4 seat cushions		
o. 10 chicken meals from the galley		

Essay Writing

Name: _____

The previous two texts (pages 28 and 30) describe two different adventures, or new experiences that had some challenges. Tell a true story about an adventure you have had by yourself, with your family, or with a friend. What did you learn from your adventure?

_____

_____

_____

_____

_____

_____

_____

_____

_____

_____

_____

_____

_____

_____

_____

_____

_____

_____

_____

_____

_____

_____

_____

_____

_____

_____

_____

Name: _____

Understanding Expository Texts

Expository texts are written to persuade someone to believe or do something. Expository writing is that in which a writer attempts to convince a reader to think a certain way. Expository writing includes any text in which the writer provides only his/her point of view. There are many different expository texts, but they all have the same purpose of trying to make someone see the point of view of the writer.

Examples of Expository Texts

essays

book reviews

political speeches and pamphlets

debates

advertisements

editorials

All expository texts have the same structure or framework. The simple exposition has four parts or paragraphs.

Expository Structure

1. An introduction is provided, in which the writer states his/her point of view on an issue.

2. The arguments for the point of view are presented.

3. The arguments against the point of view are examined.

4. A conclusion is given.

The example below follows this structure. Each section is a new paragraph.

Yellow Cars

Many car accidents happen at night or in low-light conditions. Cars that are painted darker colors, such as red, black, green, and blue, are harder to see in the dark. This makes these cars more likely to be involved in accidents. Car makers should be made to paint cars in highly noticeable colors.

Scientific research has shown that yellow is the easiest color to see, especially in low-light conditions. A sensible solution to reducing car accidents would be to paint all cars yellow. Yellow cars would show up well under streetlights and in the headlights of other vehicles, thus reducing accidents.

Many would argue that to have all cars painted yellow would make them unattractive and confuse people looking for their vehicles in large parking lots. In addition, it would make it harder to catch car thieves. There would also be many displeased car owners who like to make their own personal color choices.

While the idea of reducing accidents by yellowing all cars is a good one, the public would not accept the idea. Drivers will have to learn to be more careful on the roads, rather than repaint their cars.

Understanding Expository Texts *(cont.)*

Name: _____

1. In the example expository text, "Yellow Cars" . . .

    a. circle the introduction,

    b. underline the arguments "for,"

    c. highlight the arguments "against,"

    d. put an X next to the conclusion.

Planning an Expository Text

Step 1: Choose a topic to write about. Find something you feel strongly about. Here are some examples. You may use them or think of your own.

- All students should get paid to go to school.

- All students should have a free choice of school subjects.

- All students should have the same amount of homework.

My topic is: _____

Step 2: Plan your writing.

What main idea do you wish to persuade others about? Write your notes below. They will become your first paragraph.

_____

_____

_____

_____

_____

_____

_____

_____

_____

Name: _____

Step 2: Plan your writing. (cont.)

Make notes on facts, ideas, and information that support your main idea or point. These notes will become your second paragraph.

_____

_____

_____

_____

_____

_____

_____

Make notes about any ideas or points that go against your main idea or point. You may want to address why these counterarguments should be rejected.

_____

_____

_____

_____

_____

_____

_____

_____

Make notes about what your final thoughts are, or suggest what might or should be done as the result of your point of view being accepted. These notes will be your last paragraph, or conclusions and summary.

_____

_____

_____

_____

_____

_____

_____

Drafting an Expository Text

Name: _____

UNIT 6

Follow these guidelines to compose your draft.

1. Write the title in the center of the page and underline it.

2. Leave a line between the title and the first paragraph.

3. Start each paragraph against the margin and leave a line after each paragraph.

4. Look at each note you made in each part of the plan. Write each note as a sentence. Do not worry about overlap, repetition, or spelling at this stage. Your only aim is to turn your notes into sentences.

5. When finished, you will have a draft with four paragraphs of sentences that will need editing.

Write your draft here. If you need more space, continue on a sheet of paper and attach it.

_____
_____
_____
_____
_____
_____
_____
_____
_____
_____
_____
_____
_____
_____
_____
_____
_____
_____
_____
_____
_____

Name: _____

Proofreading and Editing a Draft

You are now ready to proofread and edit your draft. Good editing is best done using a checklist so that you can systematically edit your work without forgetting important things.

Follow these steps as you edit the draft you have just completed.

- ☐ Review each paragraph.

- ☐ Read your sentences and check that you do not have any of them in the wrong part of the text framework.

- ☐ Check that each sentence contains only one thought.

- ☐ Check for repetitions of words or ideas. Join sentences if needed, or shorten them if too long.

- ☐ When reviewing your sentences, think about the words that you have used. Can you think of better words to replace those you have used too often or to replace words that are not interesting?

- ☐ Check the capitalization and punctuation, including periods and commas.

- ☐ Check your spelling.

- ☐ Read what you have edited carefully. Ask yourself, "Does what I have written make sense?"

Hint: When proofreading your work, read what you have written aloud to yourself. You will find more errors this way.

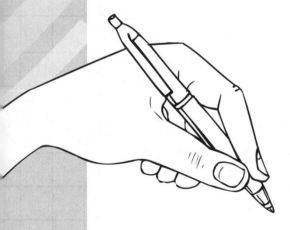

Writing the Presentation Copy

Name: _____

Just as all good writers take the time to plan, draft, and carefully edit their writing, they also take pride in their work. They make sure that the final work they present to others is arranged neatly, without any of the changes made in editing left on the page.

Write your final copy below. When you have finished it, attach it to your draft.

_____

_____

_____

_____

_____

_____

_____

_____

_____

_____

_____

_____

_____

_____

_____

_____

_____

_____

_____

_____

_____

_____

_____

_____

_____

Reading for Information

The text below contains a lot of information. Read it carefully and underline the important ideas.

It Is Dark Out There

1. When you look at the sky on a clear night, you can see thousands of stars shining. The stars we see are suns, just like our own, but they are so far away that their light is faint and they seem small.

2. There are billions of stars in our galaxy and billions of galaxies. No one knows just how many stars are in the universe. All the stars, planets, comets, and other things that we see are called "bright matter," because they can be seen through telescopes. However, that is not all there is out in space.

3. Scientists have found what they call "dark matter." This is matter that cannot be seen by telescopes. Particles of dark matter only show up because they change the way other rays of energy come to us from the center of the galaxy.

4. Scientists think that dark matter exists because its gravity affects the way galaxies hold together across the vast distances of space. These scientists believe that there is seven times more dark matter in the universe than there is bright matter.

5. No one really knows what dark matter is made up of. Until recently, it had not been detected, so it is thought to be made up of strange particles. All scientists know is that dark matter feels the pull of gravity in the same way as the matter we can see.

6. Different theories have been put forth to explain where dark matter may come from. The explosion of huge stars and black holes are just two of many theories on the origin of dark matter. Scientists exploring the idea of dark matter think that it may be a form of particle that weighs much less than a photon (the smallest unit of light that we measure).

7. If dark matter really is made up of such light particles, every cubic inch of space in the immediate vicinity of Earth must contain a lot of them. So scientists should be able to detect them in lab-based experiments. Using the European Space Agency gamma ray telescope, researchers hope to find the answer to this mystery of the universe.

Showing Understanding

1. In the grid on page 39, check true (**T**), false (**F**), or not enough evidence (**NE**) for each statement. Write the paragraph number (**PN**) that shows whether each statement is true, false, or that there is not enough evidence to decide. One has been done for you.

Showing Understanding *(cont.)* Name: _____

UNIT 7

Statement	T	F	NE	PN
a. Our sun is a star.	✔			
b. There is 17 times more dark matter than bright matter in the universe.				
c. There are many ideas explaining dark matter.				
d. Only a few scientists know what dark matter is made of.				
e. Dark matter can only be seen by telescopes.				
f. Dark matter comes from black holes.				
g. The gamma ray telescope may help researchers.				
h. Dark matter does not weigh much.				
i. Dark matter feels the pull of gravity.				
j. Bright matter includes comets.				

Incorrect to Correct

1. The statements below about dark matter are incorrect. Rewrite them so they are correct.

   a. There are millions of stars in the galaxy.

   _____

   _____

   _____

   b. Scientists think that dark matter may be a form of rock.

   _____

   _____

   _____

   c. The gravity of dark matter does not help hold the galaxy together.

   _____

   _____

   _____

   d. Particles of dark matter show up because they change as they travel.

   _____

   _____

   _____

Name: _____

Selecting the Main Idea

All well-written paragraphs have one main idea or topic. The main idea is usually found in the topic sentence. This is usually the first sentence in the paragraph, and all other sentences in the paragraph relate to it.

Note-taking

Good note-taking is based on understanding the main idea and being able to paraphrase it, or write it in your own words.

One way to find the main idea is to look for the most used noun or pronoun (i.e., a word that is the name of a thing or a word that stands for the name of a thing). Usually, that is what the topic is.

In the example that follows, some selected nouns and pronouns are boldfaced.

> The **automobile** is one of the greatest inventions of all time. **It** can carry us long distances quickly. The **automobile** is used to transport many of the things that we need from where they are made to where we live and use them. **Automobiles** have, in 100 years, gone from **carts** with unreliable **engines** that could only be used at certain times of the day, to super-fast **vehicles** that may be used night or day, on or off roads. Compared to what **they** used to cost when **automobiles** first appeared at the turn of the 20th century, the modern **automobile** is considerably cheaper, more reliable, and more useful in what **it** is able to do.

The noun *automobile* and pronouns such as *it*, which refers to *automobile*, are the most stated nouns and pronouns in this paragraph. This paragraph is about automobiles. The main idea is how automobiles have changed over the years.

1. Read the paragraphs on the following pages and look for the nouns and pronouns most used. Write the main idea of each paragraph. Use your dictionary to find the meanings of any words you do not know.

---

a. Although *T. rex* was not the largest meat-eating dinosaur, and could not run fast, it has the reputation of being the fiercest dinosaur. The long, sharp, tough teeth of the *Tyrannosaurus* made it a deadly hunter. *T. rex* has become symbolic of all dinosaurs, yet the fact is that the majority of dinosaurs were plant-eating and probably fairly docile animals.

noun/pronoun: _____

main idea: _____

_____

---

b. Earth-based telescopes are at a disadvantage by the atmosphere when looking into space. The atmosphere is a thick covering of gases that surrounds the planet. It distorts the lightwaves that travel through it. In the lower levels, rain clouds, smoke, and pollutants also cause problems for observers. For this reason, most telescopes are placed away from cities, on mountains, or in deserts where the air is cleaner and there is less atmospheric distortion.

noun/pronoun: _____

main idea: _____

_____

Selecting the Main Idea (cont.) Name: _____

c. In the short space of 100 years, modern societies have become totally dependent on electricity. Every facet of our lives is affected by electricity. It lights and heats our homes, schools, and offices. Computers now run our banks, traffic lights, telephones, cars, and communication industries. A break in the supply of electricity for any length of time brings chaos. Have we become too dependent on this marvelous source of energy?

noun/pronoun: _____

main idea: _____

_____

d. People have often pondered the question of whether we are alone in the universe. For many centuries, most people thought that Earth was the only world with living beings. In recent years, with the discovery of other planets orbiting other suns in the galaxy, the question has become more serious. Space probes have gone out into space with messages on them. Radio telescopes monitor radio waves from other star systems. Robotic machines have been sent to Mars to search for signs of life. All of these things are being done because, now, we believe that there are probably other living creatures in space.

noun/pronoun: _____

main idea: _____

_____

e. Crusoe was alone on the island. He had been alone for many years with only a parrot and some goats for company. He had not spoken to anyone except himself. He was lonely and craved some human companionship. Once, he saw a ship far out to sea, but the crew did not see his signal fire. He was convinced that he would spend his life completely alone. Being alone could do strange things to a man. It could make him see things that were not really there.

noun/pronoun: _____

main idea: _____

_____

f. As Robin approached the narrow bridge, he was surprised to see a giant of a man step onto it at the other end. He was about seven-feet tall with long, strong arms. In his right hand, he carried a long staff that looked as though it was a tree plucked out of the ground. He wore a leather cap on his head and a leather vest on his chest. As he walked, the log bridge buckled with his weight. Robin continued over the log from his side.

noun/pronoun: _____

main idea: _____

_____

Name: _____

Note-Taking and Topic Sentences

More and more often you will be asked to read texts and make notes or summaries of their content. You will be required to learn and remember information. Having a procedure to follow will help you read, take notes, and make summaries. One way of doing this is to use the topic sentence summary approach. This approach or procedure is simple, quick, and easy to remember.

As each step is explained, use the text titled "It Is Dark Out There" on page 38 to complete it.

Step #1: Read the text. As you read, highlight each topic sentence (usually the first sentence of each paragraph).

Step #2: Make topic sentence headings. Write each topic sentence or a brief statement of the main idea. There are seven paragraphs to be recorded.

_____

_____

_____

_____

_____

_____

Step #3: Read the text again. Write a question for each topic sentence. For example, "What can be seen as you look into the night sky?"

_____

_____

_____

_____

_____

Step #4: Check what you have written. If you have all you need, you can keep these summaries as notes. From now on, you should use these notes.

Step #5: Follow these steps for memorization. (You may wish to remember these notes for test-taking or some other reason.)

1. Read your notes once.

2. Cover them up and try to write them out on paper.

3. Check your attempt and write in the missing parts. Throw this attempt away and try again.

4. Repeat steps 1 to 3 until you can rewrite your notes without needing to correct your attempt.

5. From time to time, revise these notes.

Understanding Text Types

Name: _____

Writers and readers go together. No readers equal no writers, and no writers equal no readers. Writers have a purpose for writing, and readers have a purpose for reading. There are two main purposes for reading and writing:

- for information

- for enjoyment

Writers use six kinds of texts to meet their purposes for writing. Read the table below, which shows the text types and their purposes. Check the text types you have read or written.

Text Type	Purpose	Examples
recount ☐	to tell about real experiences or happenings in the order that they happened (nonfiction)	personal experiences, diaries, journals, logs, histories, biographies, true stories, some poems, some documentary movies, legends
narrative ☐	to entertain by using fiction	novels, plays, some poems, some movies, short stories, myths, made-up stories
report ☐	to classify, describe, locate, and present the dynamic qualities of living and non-living things	descriptions of things (e.g., animals, plants, machines, buildings)
procedure ☐	to describe how something is done	handbooks, manuals, recipes, do-it-yourself guides, steps for doing things (e.g., solving math problems)
explanation ☐	to explain what things or processes are and how they work	why it is dark at night
expository ☐	to persuade, argue, criticize, give reasons why things should be done, or give an opinion	book reviews, debates, speeches, documentaries

1. What type of text would be used for these purposes?

   a. Telling a friend about an accident you witnessed

   _____

   b. Trying to convince your friend to join a travel trip you think would be good to experience

   _____

   c. Describing how to take a photograph

   _____

Name: _____

Determining Text Types

1. Examine the titles below. Refer to the table on the previous page and write what each kind of text is in the box.

Book Title	Type of Text
a. *A Guide to Making Things with Wood*	
b. *The Grizzly Bear*	
c. *The Life of Steve Jobs*	
d. *The Mystery of Bigfoot*	
e. *How a Computer Works*	
f. *The Need for Changes in Education*	
g. *My Trip to Europe*	
h. *The Adventures of Pickle Pig*	
i. *The Schoolboy's Cookbook*	
j. *About Tyrannosaurus rex*	
k. *The Early Life of Abraham Lincoln*	
l. *Submarines: What They Are and How They Operate*	
m. *The Poem of the Pied Piper*	
n. *The Secret Adventures of the "Spy Kids"*	
o. *How to Make a Kite*	
p. *Arguments for Reducing Taxation*	
q. *A Brief History of China*	
r. *Making a Go-Kart*	
s. *Dolphins*	
t. *Reasons for Having No Homework*	
u. *The Day I Went Horseriding*	
v. *The Story of the Fox and the Crow*	
w. *Cooking for Fun*	
x. *The Adventures of Robinson Crusoe*	
y. *Science Experiments*	
z. *Why Running Is Good for Your Health*	

44

Finding the Author's Purpose   Name: _____

Texts are written for a particular purpose. These include:

1. to entertain
2. to describe how something is done
3. to classify and describe a thing
4. to criticize and review
5. to explain how something works
6. to give an account of an experience

1. Write the correct number next to each text below to show its purpose. The first one has been done for you.

a. While we waited for our baggage at the airport in Rome, I saw an old school friend I hadn't seen for years. He was also traveling through Italy. | **6**

b. The platypus is unlike other animals. It has a large, duck-like, flexible beak on a small head. The front of its long, sleek body is covered with fur.

c. After removing all the nuts from the hub of the wheel, gently lift the wheel off the axle and place it to one side. Next, put the spare wheel on the hub and loosely screw on two wheel nuts to hold the wheel in place while you put the remaining nuts on.

d. An elephant drinking at the Zambezi River noticed a turtle asleep on a log. He ambled over and kicked the turtle right across the river.

"Why did you do that?" asked a passing rhino.

"I recognized it as the same one that bit my trunk 55 years ago," the elephant replied.

"Amazing! What a memory you have," said the passing rhino.

"Yes, I have turtle recall."

e. *A Frog in My Soup* by Bob Croaker is not as enjoyable as his earlier books about the adventures of Swamp Kid and his pet frog. The book lacks a good storyline and is hard to follow in places.

f. A submarine is a ship designed to go beneath the surface of the water. In order to do this, the submarine must fill large tanks with water so that it sinks rather than floats. To rise up out of the water, compressed air forces the water out of the tanks.

g. The Sydney Opera House is a large entertainment center. The complex is an unusual design that gives the appearance of sails. Within the complex are many venues that are used to seat audiences and rehearse performances. It also houses offices and other administrative facilities.

Name: _____

Determining the Purpose

Read the following Aboriginal Australian myth to determine the purpose of the story.

Min-Na-Wee (Why the Crocodile Rolls)

The people of the group were almost always happy. There was plenty of food to be found along the coast and time for work and play. Everyone was happy—except little Min-na-wee.

Min-na-wee was a little girl who liked making trouble among the other little girls. She often caused fights between the girls and their mothers.

The older people of the group knew of Min-na-wee's desire to cause trouble. They warned Min-na-wee's mother that if she did not stop her daughter from causing trouble, then something terrible would happen to Min-na-wee.

Years passed and even when Min-na-wee became a young woman, she still liked to cause trouble. One day, all the young women, including Min-na-wee, stood in a line to be selected as brides. The elders pointed out which men were to marry which women. At the end of the ceremony, only Min-na-wee was left standing there. She had not been picked to become a wife.

Min-na-wee became even more troublesome. She caused fights every day. Pleased with herself, Min-na-wee sat back and watched the fights.

The old people of the tribe agreed that Min-na-wee had to be punished for what she had done. Min-na-wee did not know of the tribe's decision. As she approached the women to cause another fight, she was grabbed by the men and rolled around and around in the dirt.

Min-na-wee managed to break free and run to the sea. There, she called on the evil spirits to make her into a savage animal so she could attack the people of the group. The spirit made Min-na-wee into a huge crocodile. She slid silently into the muddy waters and waited.

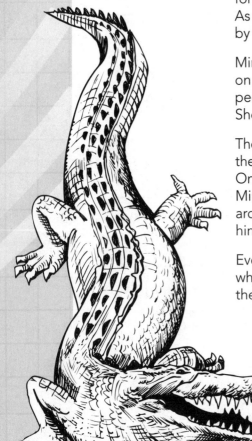

The people soon forgot Min-na-wee as they went about their daily tasks. As they walked along the banks, hunting for mudcrabs, Min-na-wee lay waiting. One of the men who had punished Min-na-wee jumped into the water. Min-na-wee swam silently behind him and grabbed him. She rolled him around and around, just like he had done to her. Over and over she rolled him in the water, until she was confident he had been punished enough.

Even today, Min-na-wee's spirit is still found among the crocodiles. This is why every time a crocodile catches its prey, it rolls it around and around in the water.

Determining the Purpose (cont.) Name: _____

1. Circle a number to show the possibility of each statement being the reason for telling the story of Min-na-wee.

high ◀━━━━━━━━ low

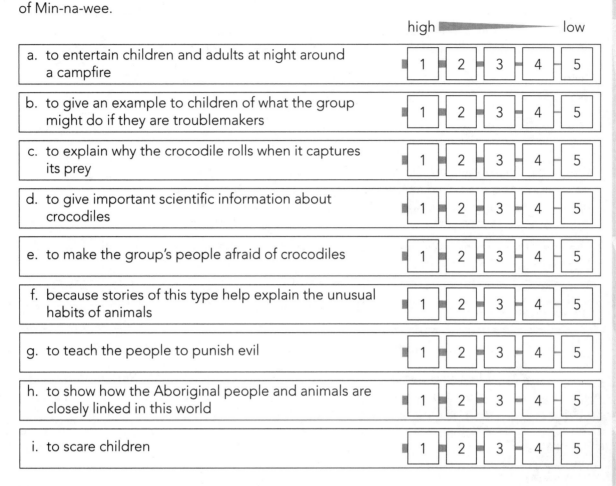

a. to entertain children and adults at night around a campfire
| 1 | 2 | 3 | 4 | 5 |

b. to give an example to children of what the group might do if they are troublemakers
| 1 | 2 | 3 | 4 | 5 |

c. to explain why the crocodile rolls when it captures its prey
| 1 | 2 | 3 | 4 | 5 |

d. to give important scientific information about crocodiles
| 1 | 2 | 3 | 4 | 5 |

e. to make the group's people afraid of crocodiles
| 1 | 2 | 3 | 4 | 5 |

f. because stories of this type help explain the unusual habits of animals
| 1 | 2 | 3 | 4 | 5 |

g. to teach the people to punish evil
| 1 | 2 | 3 | 4 | 5 |

h. to show how the Aboriginal people and animals are closely linked in this world
| 1 | 2 | 3 | 4 | 5 |

i. to scare children
| 1 | 2 | 3 | 4 | 5 |

Recognizing a Narrative

The story of Min-na-wee is a narrative. A narrative text tells about events that happen over time, but, unlike a recount, they are not true.

All narratives have the same basic structure. Read the information about narrative text structure and the example below and on the next page.

Robin and the Beggar

One day, Robin met an old beggar on the road through the forest. "Where are you going?" asked Robin. The beggar replied that he was going to the archery contest because the sheriff was giving a bag of gold to the winner.	**Exposition** (who, when, where, why)
Robin gave the beggar a gold coin. "Swap clothes with me!" Robin told the beggar.	**Initiating event** (what causes the action or events)
In Nottingham, no one recognized Robin as the scruffy, old beggar with the limp. When Robin entered the contest, everyone laughed.	**Complication** (the start of conflict or difficulty)

Robin and the Beggar *(cont.)*

In each round, the old beggar managed to stay in the contest until there were only two contestants left: the beggar and the sheriff's best archer. "Move the target back 50 feet," said the beggar. "It's too close for my old eyes to see." The sheriff's archer was a good shot, and all three of his arrows landed on the distant target. The sheriff was pleased. When the old beggar came to shoot, he seemed to have trouble standing up straight, and the crowd laughed. They stopped laughing as the beggar's three arrows all landed in the very center of the target.	**Events** (the events in time order that the main characters work through to overcome the problems or conflict)
The sheriff reluctantly gave the beggar the bag of gold. "Where did you learn to shoot like that?" the sheriff asked.	**Resolution**
"A man called Robin Hood taught me," replied the beggar.	**Ending**

A simple narrative may have only three parts: exposition, middle, and an ending.

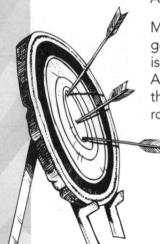

Many jokes are simple narratives. Stories such as "Little Red Riding Hood" are good examples of narratives. One of the best ways to begin writing a narrative is to take a well-known story and rewrite it using your own characters and ideas. Another way is to take an adventure you have had and add in people and events that you create. For example, a simple visit to the mall can become a bank-robber chase.

Planning and Writing a Narrative

One of the best ways to begin writing narratives is to tell a story to a friend or small group. Use the story organizer below to plan your narrative.

Step #1: Planning

	Example	Your Plan
Exposition	One night, a man loses his money so he decides to rob the king's treasury.	

Planning and Writing a Narrative (cont.)

Name: _____

	Example	Your Plan
Initiating Event	The palace guards capture him and take him to the king.	
Complication	The king finds him guilty and says that his court magician will turn him into one of two things: a prime-rib steak or a pork chop. He can choose between the two options.	
Event #1	The man thinks for a moment and says he would prefer to be turned into prime rib.	
Event #2	The king and all the court are amazed, since no one ever chooses this option. The king asks the man why he wants to be turned into steak.	
Resolution/ Ending	The man replies, "A hot steak is better than a cold chop."	

Step #2: Telling the story

Using your notes, tell your story to a classmate or group of students. The more times you tell it, the better it will become. After telling it two or three times, you will have it right. When you write your story as you have told it to your classmate/group, it will make sense and you will be able to write it down without too much difficulty.

Step #3: Writing the draft

Use your story organizer notes and the sentences you used when you told your story to write a draft narrative. Write your draft on a sheet of paper and attach it to this page.

Step #4: Proofreading and editing

Proofread your work following the guidelines you were given on page 36.

Step #5: Presenting your narrative

Write your final copy. Follow the guidelines on page 36. Write the final copy of your narrative on a sheet of paper and attach it.

Name: _____

All About Context Clues

A context clue allows the reader to understand words and ideas with which they are not familiar. There are several different types of context clues.

Definition

A word or phrase that has been defined by the author

Example: A chimera is <u>a mythical creature with body parts from various animals</u>.

Synonym

A word or phrase that shares the same meaning with another word or phrase

Example: We all agreed that the <u>spicy</u> tomato soup was very <u>savory</u>.

Antonym

A word or phrase that shares the opposite meaning with another word or phrase

Example: The gorilla is often <u>gentle</u>, but it can also be <u>ferocious</u>.

Example

Words or phrases used as examples to illustrate the subject of the sentence

Example: <u>Constellations</u>, like the famous group of stars named Orion, can be seen on a clear night.

Write sample sentences for each of the four types of context clues.

1. Definition: _____

   _____

2. Definition: _____

   _____

3. Synonym: _____

   _____

4. Synonym: _____

   _____

5. Antonym: _____

   _____

6. Antonym: _____

   _____

7. Example: _____

   _____

8. Example: _____

   _____

Using Context Clues

Name: _____

The context in reading refers to the overall meaning of the text. The context gives us clues about the words we read.

1. Read the two sentences and write the words needed to complete them.

   a. The hungry spider _____ the juicy fly.

   (With a knowledge, that is, context, of spiders and flies, the reader would be likely to predict that the missing word is "ate.")

   b. The loving mother _____ the hungry baby.

   (With a knowledge, that is, context, of mothers and babies, the reader would be likely to predict that the missing word is "fed.")

2. Write the meaning of each of the nonsense words by reading the contexts.

   a. **Nusters**
      *   *Nusters* are useful to wear when the weather is cold.
      *   Some *nusters* are waterproof.
      *   There are different types of *nusters* for different occasions.
      *   Some houses have a special closet near the front door where visitors can hang their *nusters*.

      Nuster means _____.

   b. **Tortum**
      *   Mother gets *tortum* when we are late for dinner.
      *   The teacher was very *tortum* when a student broke the computer.
      *   As people get older, they usually learn to control their *tortum* moments.
      *   A *tortum* person does not think as clearly as a non-*tortum* person.

      Tortum means _____.

   c. **Keshlons**
      *   *Keshlons* live in Africa.
      *   *Keshlons* are very large.
      *   *Keshlons* eat a large amount of grass and other plants.
      *   *Keshlons* have horns on their noses.

      Keshlon means _____.

   d. **Zingling**
      *   Too much *zingling* will make you tired.
      *   Some people go *zingling* for exercise.
      *   *Zingling* is a faster way of going from one place to another.

      Zingling means _____.

Name: _____

Use the words in the box to complete the text.

Biggest Mammal

Earth	special	reasons	seafood	room
baleen	sea	consists	krill	ancient
whale	tremendously	water	ocean	

A blue whale's diet _____ mostly of krill, a tiny crustacean
1

that lives in _____ large numbers in almost every
2

_____ in the world.
3

Krill is one of the most plentiful food species (apart from insects) anywhere on

_____. The blue whale has a big appetite. A big blue whale
4

can eat over a thousand _____ at one time by swallowing them.
5

The tongue of a blue whale weighs as much as an elephant!

Blue whales eat the krill using a _____ type of filter on their
6

mouths called a "baleen." The blue whale gulps enormous amounts of sea

_____ containing live krill, then closes its mouth and flushes the
7

sea water back out through the _____, leaving the krill behind.
8

Small fish and plankton are also favorite foods of the _____.
9

It takes about 4 tons of fresh _____ a day to keep a blue whale
10

well fed.

Scientists don't really know for sure why the blue whale is so big. However,

they are sure of one thing; as big as the _____ dinosaurs
11

were, they were never as big as the blue whale. One of the most important

_____ why blue whales have become so large is that they
12

have more space—more _____ to roam. Remember, over
13

70% of Earth is covered in _____ water.
14

Using Context to Get Meaning

Name: _____

Read this text. It has a nonsense word in it.

A hungry **gloop** saw a banana tree. The **gloop** climbed the tree and ate a banana.

Instead of the word "gloop" you could write the word "monkey" and the text would make sense.

1. Rewrite the texts below, putting real words in the place of the nonsense words. Remember, you can put in any word you wish so long as what you write makes sense. If the same nonsense word is used more than once in a text, it must be replaced by the same new word each time.

   a. Once upon a fibble, a little old dult built a house out of tin cans.

   _____

   _____

   b. A dimsey snigle hugged a loga.

   _____

   _____

   c. Fourteen snurples and six snurples make zinty snurples.

   _____

   _____

   d. There was once a ging who lived in a large wasalace all by himself. He was very grongy and wanted some felter to be his wife. Sadly, there was no one that would yonter him because he was too lazy.

   _____

   _____

   _____

   _____

   e. Juntz upon a pime a doggen slonked into a grabbet. He was grolling for neft because he was klombly. He grolled and grolled until he spotted a turkon.

   "Do yum fow where I can gine some neft?" he asked the turkon.

   _____

   _____

   _____

   _____

Name: _____

Reading Maps and Keys

Use the city map and key below to answer the questions and solve the problems on the next page.

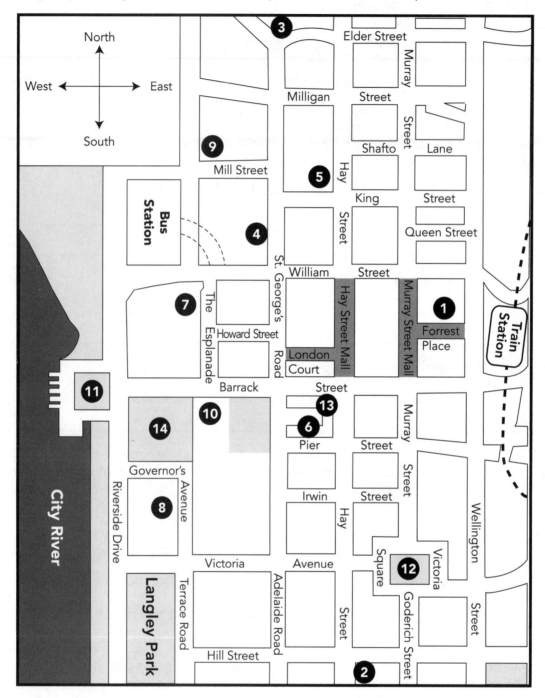

1. Post Office	7. Allan Green Observatory	13. Town Hall
2. City Mint	8. Governor's House	14. Supreme Court and Gardens
3. The Barracks Arch	9. Old Mill Museum	▉ Mall
4. Old City Boy's School	10. City Barracks	– – rail line
5. The Royal Theater	11. Barrack Square and Bell Tower	▨ gardens/parks
6. St. George's Cathedral	12. St. Mary's Cathedral	⋯ overpass

Reading Maps and Keys *(cont.)* Name: _____

Answer the following questions by giving your answers in the same way as this example.

Question: What is the shortest way to go from the corner of Hay and Elder streets to Queen Street?

Answer: East on Elder for one block, then south on Murray for four blocks.

1. Give the directions for the shortest routes between these places.

   a. The Post Office to the City Mint

   _____

   _____

   b. The Barracks Arch to the Old City Boy's School

   _____

   _____

   c. From the train station to The Royal Theater

   _____

   _____

   d. From the bus station to St. George's Cathedral

   _____

   _____

2. Answer these questions.

   a. What are the names of the streets that connect Riverside Drive and Wellington Street?

   _____

   b. Give the name and location of a good place to find new coins.

   _____

   c. Give the name and location of a good place to see stars.

   _____

   d. Which streets are named after a queen?

   _____

3. Give reasons why these streets are named as they are.

   a. Mill Street

   b. Barrack Street

   c. Governor's Avenue

Name: _____

Interpreting a Map

1. Use the city map and key on page 54 to determine whether each statement below is true (**T**), false (**F**), or there is not enough evidence (**NE**) to decide. Check the appropriate boxes.

Statement	T	F	NE
a. King Street is longer than Queen Street.			
b. There are more shops on William Street than on Barrack Street.			
c. The Governor's House is north of London Court.			
d. The bell tower is 65 feet high.			
e. It is not possible to go from the corner of Shafto Lane and Murray Street to Victoria Square without leaving Murray Street.			
f. Girls were once educated in a school on St. George's Road.			
g. St. Mary's Cathedral is completely surrounded by streets.			
h. Hay Street runs north to south.			
i. The Town Hall is on Barrack Street.			
j. The City River is close to Riverside Drive.			
k. Victoria Avenue is five blocks long.			
l. The Supreme Court and Gardens are near the river.			
m. Mill Street is named after a flour mill.			
n. The quickest way from the bus station to the train station is along William Street.			
o. The governor has a view of the river.			
p. Hill Street is north of Elder Street.			
q. You can send a letter at Forrest Place.			
r. Hay Street is west of Murray Street.			
s. The Old City Boy's School is now an art gallery.			
t. The Royal Theater is on the corner of Hay Street and King Street.			

Personalized Maps

Name: _____

Create a map of your school or neighborhood. Then add a key to indicate where specific places are located.

The life of Marco Polo is one of the most interesting adventures. The following text presents some of his experiences.

This text is part of a recount. As you read, think about the difficulties that you would face going on such a journey in those times.

The Adventures of Marco Polo

1. Probably the best-known westerner to travel the famous Silk Road from Europe to China was Marco Polo (1254–1324). His fame results from a number of factors. He was a very determined person who wrote widely of his experiences. He also had influence in the court of the Khan (great chief of Mongol tribes). His Asian odyssey lasted 24 years and took him farther, in dangerous times, than any previous traveler. He became a friend of the great Kublai Khan (1214–1294). He traveled the length and breadth of China. More importantly, he was able to return to Europe to tell the greatest travel story of the time.

2. Marco Polo's family were nobles who originated on the coast of Dalmatia (Croatia). Brothers Niccolo and Mafeo had a trading post on an island in the Adriatic Sea. Venice (Italy), where young Marco grew up, was at that time the trade and business center of the Mediterranean. Marco was educated as the son of a wealthy man—he spoke business French as well as Italian, studied the classics, and showed an interest in nature, in people, and in strange and intriguing animals.

3. When his father and uncle left Venice for their first trip to Cathay (China), Marco was just 6 years old. He would turn 15 before they returned! His mother had died while his father was away. Marco stayed with his father and uncle for more than two years before the three of them left for a second major expedition to China.

4. By now, it was late 1271. Armed with letters and presents from Pope Gregory X, the now 17-year-old Marco left Venice for China with his father and uncle. They took two friars with them—who promptly turned around and headed home when they found themselves in a battle zone! Wanting to avoid using the same route they had used more than a decade earlier, the Polos traveled through Armenia, Persia (Iran), Afghanistan, and on to China and Mongolia.

5. Marco's adventures were simply amazing, and he faithfully recorded the strange places and events he experienced. What he had to say about the great Gobi Desert of China and Mongolia gives us some insight into his feelings for the huge size of the place, as well as his admiration for those who regularly crossed it.

6. "This desert is reported to be so long that it would take a year to go from end to end; and at the narrowest point, it takes a month to cross it. It consists entirely of mountains and sands and valleys. There is nothing at all to eat." Even though the desert was dangerous, Marco's reports indicate that trade routes across it were well traveled at this time. Of course, the desert wasn't entirely without dangers of its own.

The Adventures of Marco Polo *(cont.)*

7. "When a man is riding through the desert by night, he may fall asleep or be distracted and become separated from his companions and want to rejoin them. He may hear spirit voices talking to him as if they were his companions. Sometimes they may even call him by name. Often these voices lure him away from the path and he never finds it again. Many travelers have become lost and died because of this.

8. "Sometimes in the night, travelers hear a noise which sounds like the clatter of a great company of riders away from the road. If they believe that these are some of their company and head for the noise, they find themselves hopelessly lost. There are some who, in crossing the desert, have seen a host of men coming towards them and, suspecting that they were robbers, they have hidden from them and gone hopelessly astray.

9. "Even by daylight, men hear these spirit voices. Often they hear the strains of many instruments, especially drums, and the clash of arms. For this reason, bands of travelers make a point of keeping very close together. Before they go to sleep, they set up a sign pointing in the direction in which they have to travel the next day. They fasten little bells round the necks of all their beasts so that by listening to the sound, they may prevent themselves from straying off the path."

"Had I not experienced it I would not have believed the half of what I saw."
—Marco Polo

Supporting Statements

1. The following statements are true interpretations or assumptions about the text "The Adventures of Marco Polo." Write a short sentence containing proof from the text. Give the paragraph number to show where you found the statement.

   a. Marco Polo was born in the middle of the 13th century.

   _____

   _____

   b. Before Marco's trip to Cathay, his uncle and father had already been there.

   _____

   _____

   c. The desert is a very large, harsh place.

   _____

   _____

Supporting Statements *(cont.)*

d. There is very little to sustain life in the desert.

_____

_____ ☐

e. Men in the desert must be constantly alert.

_____

_____ ☐

f. Desert travelers often suffer hallucinations.

_____

_____ ☐

g. The main road through the desert was well used by the time Marco traveled it.

_____

_____ ☐

h. Thieves and bandits were often found in the desert.

_____

_____ ☐

Completing an Event Grid

1. Connect the person or place with the comments. Write a paragraph number that shows where the connection can be found. The first one has been done for you.

	Kublai Khan	Desert	Marco Polo	Father and Uncle
a. experienced travelers				3
b. an intelligent man				
c. harsh				
d. arid				
e. courageous				
f. Chief of Mongol tribes				
g. unusual voices				
h. from a noble family				
i. merchants				
j. knew French and Italian				
k. journey lasted 24 years				
l. 1214–1294				
m. strange sights				
n. born 1254				

Thinking Critically

Name: _____

1. In this activity you will work in groups of five or six. Complete the activity individually first, then discuss it as a group. Write a group response in the last column.

Desert Journey

You are journeying home and are about to cross the Gobi Desert when your party is attacked by robbers. All except you are mortally wounded. You manage to find a camel, a small packhorse, and the items listed below.

Select the items essential for your survival in the desert for a trip that will last about a year. A camel can carry about 330 lbs. and a small horse about 200 lbs. without being overloaded. You are able to carry 44 lbs. as you walk. Keep a tally of the weight of the items you choose so the weight is not more than can be carried. Put an X in the "rank" column to indicate items you had to leave behind.

Item	Weight (lbs.)	Your Rank	Group Rank
a. sword	4		
b. 4 blankets	9		
c. large bag of dried fruit	55		
d. 40-foot-long rope	7		
e. bow and quiver of arrows	24		
f. 2 leather pouches of dried meat	88		
g. 5 gallons of water	165		
h. extra sets of clothes	37		
i. tent	44		
j. telescope	11		
k. bucket to collect camel's milk/water	7		
l. 4 large water bottles	35		
m. firewood	132		
n. sleeping bag	10		
o. map of the desert road	1		
p. knife	1		
q. cooking pot and spoon	3		
r. fresh fruit	26		
s. horse feed	77		

Name: _____

Associating Word Meanings

1. Circle the words associated with the keywords on the left. You may need a dictionary to help you.

Keywords	Associated Words				
a. desert	barren	harsh	moist	sand	forest
b. oasis	grass	salt	water	plants	camp
c. camel	strong	herbivore	friendly	hump	nasty
d. Khan	ruler	powerful	ruthless	ignorant	warrior
e. Mongols	horsemen	fierce	yurts	tribal	afraid
f. Venice	merchants	sea	English	trade	warlike
g. Marco Polo	Persia	America	Armenia	Venice	France
h. hallucinate	eerie	strange	helpful	imagined	old
i. horse	carnivore	saddle	strong	extinct	tame
j. ship	crew	mast	sail	cargo	wings
k. trade	goods	money	merchants	banks	charity
l. yurt	tent	large	shelter	bricks	felt
m. traveler	horse	ship	plane	farm	road
n. mountains	forests	lakes	rocks	slopes	snow
o. sea	water	ships	trade	dry	storms

Wrong to Right

1. In each sentence below, the underlined word is not correct for the adventures of Marco Polo. Replace it with a word that makes the statement true.

   a. Marco told of common things and places.

   new word: _____

   b. Marco was an old man when he began his journey.

   new word: _____

   c. Marco had a poor knowledge of languages.

   new word: _____

   d. The route through the desert was unestablished when Marco traveled it.

   new word: _____

Matching Terms and Definitions

Name: _____

1. Write the letter of the definition alongside the correct term.

☐ compass   ☐ electric shovel   ☐ spark plug

☐ cherry picker   ☐ monorail   ☐ jet ski

☐ electric drill   ☐ jackhammer   ☐ scuba tanks

☐ vault   ☐ periscope   ☐ Mars Rover

☐ generator   ☐ satellite

☐ extension ladder ☐ circular saw

	Definitions
a.	a secure place for the storage of valuable items
b.	a transport system using a single track
c.	a large mechanical device for mining large quantities of ore
d.	a device that provides an adjustable platform to work in high and awkward places
e.	a climbing device that can be reduced in length for easy carrying and storage
f.	air cylinders that provide air for underwater work
g.	a self-propelled device for exploring planetary surfaces
h.	a device that allows a viewer to see objects from a higher perspective
i.	a tool for the destruction of masonry
j.	a device for ignition through the discharging of electricity in the form of an electrical arc
k.	a direction-pointing device based on Earth's magnetism
l.	a device for making holes in various materials
m.	a craft that skims rapidly over water
n.	a device that, when turned rapidly, produces electricity
o.	an object that orbits another object
p.	a device for cutting timber or other materials

Name: _____

Interpreting Pictures

1. Examine the image below. Then write **T** (true), **F** (false), **PT** (probably true), **PF** (probably false), or **NE** (no evidence) for each comment.

a. Some buildings are more damaged than others. _____

b. All the buildings are houses. _____

c. The man standing outside the garage doorway of the top left-hand house is the mayor. _____

d. The damage was caused by a tornado. _____

e. There is some fire damage to the house in the bottom left-hand corner. _____

f. All the cars are rescue vehicles. _____

g. An old lady is hiding in the basement of one of the houses. _____

h. A gas explosion tore the roofs from the houses. _____

i. Some buildings are undamaged. _____

j. The disaster happened at night. _____

k. The insurance bill will be enormous. _____

l. No one escaped the destruction alive. _____

Using Guided Reading for a Recount

Name: _____

Read the recount that describes what happened when a tornado struck some houses in a small town in Victoria, Australia. As you read, try to imagine your feelings if you were there. What would you do? How would you behave?

A Tornado Strikes

One quiet Sunday afternoon in May 2003, the people in a small rural town in Victoria, Australia, went about their various tasks. Some were on the streets talking, others were cooking dinner, some were socializing at small parties, while others were coming home from work. Suddenly, some of the people saw a large, black cloud moving quickly towards them. Some of those who watched saw the long tail coming from the cloud and knew, because they had seen the movie *Twister*, that it was a tornado.

The storm, described by the Weather Bureau as an F2-class tornado—one of the worst experienced in Victoria—approached the town of Eaglehawk just before 6 p.m. It appeared to strike first on a field near Watson Avenue. The van of a Mr. Ashwell was picked up and flung about 500 feet into a neighbor's yard.

Local high-school principal Phil Britton was at home with his 83-year-old mother, Gwen, when he heard a "strange noise" approaching. He looked out the window and saw the tornado coming straight for the house. It came across the yard in front of his house—a gray, swirling mass with a roar like a locomotive and with all kinds of objects whirling in it. In less than a second, furniture under the carport of the house next door got picked up and hurled over the road, smashing the Brittons' window. All at once, bits of broken glass went flying around. The roof was torn off, and all the insulation in the ceiling fell down, like snow in a snowstorm.

One resident, working in his garage with the door open, looked up and saw sheets of roofing, pieces of wood, branches of trees, and other garbage—including the door of a car—swirling around in the air about 100–130 feet up. "It was like a huge, dark whirlpool with things being tossed around as if they were in a washing machine."

A local schoolteacher, who had just arrived home from a day on a nearby farm, was cooking a meal when the tornado struck. "I thought it was a plane coming to land on my house. The roaring was terrible and frightening," she said. Strangely, her house was spared while that of her neighbors, who were away for the weekend, was flattened and all their personal belongings scattered over a great distance.

In the next few minutes, the tornado whipped through the town, destroying 10 homes and extensively damaging at least 50 others.

A Tornado Strikes (cont.)

The three-year-old home of a couple near Mr. Britton's house was also totally wrecked. They arrived back from church to be confronted with the devastation of their house. "Church was the safest place to be in a time like this," said the young couple.

When the tornado swooped on its path of destruction, it ripped the roof from another home and deposited it high in the trees across the road. The owner of the house heard a roar from behind his block and watched as the roof was peeled off the house next door.

On the other side of the road, a woman was roasting a chicken for dinner when the power was cut. Her sons, 11 and 7, ran in from the front room. They were screaming because there were windows breaking and glass smashing everywhere. Their mother grabbed them. One of the boys was hysterical and had opened the door to get out, but she managed to drag him back. The woman then went to go to the basement of the 140-year-old home, but before she could get there, it was all over.

When they went outside, they found the entire roof of the historical home had disappeared. The beautiful garden with its tall, old trees, including a 100-year-old magnolia, looked as though it had been put through a shredder.

The State Emergency Service got close to 130 calls for help in the period after the storm. The tornado was not systematic in its destruction. It seemed almost playful, slashing through some dwellings while leaving neighboring houses almost untouched.

The next day, over 70 S.E.S. volunteers from 11 units helped repair damaged houses. Those living in the town tried to make some sense out of the short but devastating natural disaster and come to terms with the cost of the damage, estimated to be many millions of dollars. The Emergency Services Minister toured the area and promised those affected would be eligible for state government grants of up to $22,800, including $900 per household for emergency assistance to buy food, clothing, and provide short-term accommodation. The Insurance Council of Australia said insured residents would be covered for wind and storm damage.

For some, however, the destruction was a more severe loss. One elderly lady of 72, whose 100-year-old timber cottage took the full force of the wind, was very upset. She felt it was the end of things for her since she had lost her husband three months before and then the tornado had done the rest. Her year had not started well and had not gotten any better.

Using Guided Reading for a Recount *(cont.)*

Name: _____

1. Use these questions to help you understand the text.

   a. Underline the main events in the narrative.

   b. List the people who gave eyewitness accounts.

   _____

   _____

   c. Write some descriptive or emotive words or phrases that added to the text.

   _____

   _____

   _____

Expanding Sentences

1. Replace the boldfaced word with two descriptive words so the sentence still makes sense. One has been done for you.

   a. The large, black cloud was **coming** towards Eaglehawk.

   The large, black cloud was hurtling swiftly towards Eaglehawk. _____

   _____

   b. The storm **approached** Eaglehawk.

   _____

   _____

   c. There were pieces of glass **flying** around.

   _____

   _____

   d. The roof of the historical home had **disappeared**.

   _____

   _____

   e. The houses in the street were **destroyed** by the storm.

   _____

   _____

   f. Water from the river **flowed** into the streets.

   _____

   _____

Name: _____

1. Read the following explanatory text and then answer the questions that relate to both it and the recount on pages 65–66.

About Tornadoes

A tornado is a rapidly moving column of air, driven by energy in the atmosphere. A tornado usually occurs in conjunction with a severe thunderstorm.

The best-known feature of a tornado is the funnel-shaped tail that reaches down to Earth from a cumulonimbus cloud. Often called a "twister," a tornado can range in size from just a few feet to a mile wide at the point that touches the ground. Most of them are fairly narrow—just 1,000 feet wide. It moves in a spectacular fashion over Earth, up to many miles in distance. But it causes massive damage whenever it touches down. The "funnel" that we see as a characteristic of tornadoes is made up of dust, dirt, and other debris, as well as condensation—when water droplets are formed in the funnel's center. This condensation is the same as what happens with the generally weaker ocean tornadoes, called waterspouts. These are found most often in tropical waters. People believe that tornadoes always spin clockwise in the southern hemisphere and counterclockwise in the northern hemisphere, but this isn't necessarily so. Some tornadoes have actually done the opposite. Land-based tornadoes occur most often—and are strongest—in the temperate zones.

Since the "average" twister is only about 500 feet in diameter where it touches down, larger versions appear much more frightening. But size is deceptive, because the size of a tornado tells us nothing about how strong it is or how much damage it is likely to cause. What is important is the difference in atmospheric pressure inside the funnel and outside. The greater the difference, the faster the winds—and the more damage they have the potential to cause.

We classify tornadoes on the Fujita Scale, which has a direct relationship with wind speed—a major factor in damage. The chart below shows how the Fujita Scale ties wind speed to damage.

Fujita Damage Scale

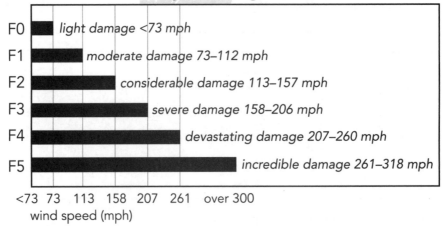

F0	light damage <73 mph
F1	moderate damage 73–112 mph
F2	considerable damage 113–157 mph
F3	severe damage 158–206 mph
F4	devastating damage 207–260 mph
F5	incredible damage 261–318 mph

<73 73 113 158 207 261   over 300
wind speed (mph)

On land, tornadoes are most likely to occur on flat plains, where there are powerful thunderstorms. Vast areas of many countries, especially in the United States, Australia, and India, meet these conditions.

Understanding Explanatory Texts *(cont.)*

Name: _____

a. Why do you think that tornadoes do the most damage on the large, flat plains of countries and not in the hilly areas?

_____

_____

_____

b. Why are tornadoes considered one of the worst natural disasters?

_____

_____

_____

Reading a Procedure Text

The following procedure covers the things to do if you are in a tornado or any other strong wind area, such as those frequented by cyclones.

What to Do to Protect Against Tornadoes

Materials Needed

The following pieces of equipment or supplies need to be gathered and stored safely and made available for easy access. This is called a "Disaster Supplies Kit."

- first aid kit and essential medications
- canned food and can opener
- at least 4 gallons of water per person
- protective clothing, bedding, or sleeping bags
- battery-powered radio, flashlight, and extra batteries
- special items for infant, elderly, or disabled family members
- written instructions on how to turn off electricity, gas, and water if authorities advise you to do so (*Remember:* You'll need a professional to turn natural gas services back on.)

Safety Steps to Complete

1. Prepare a home tornado plan.
   - Select a place where your family could gather when a tornado is headed your way. It could be your basement, or, if you have no basement, a central hallway, bathroom, or built-in wardrobe on the lowest floor. Keep this place uncluttered.
   - If you are in a high-rise building, you may not have enough time to go to the lowest floor. Pick a place in a hallway in the center of the building.

2. Stay tuned for warnings.
    - Listen to your local radio and TV stations for updated information.
    - Know what a tornado **watch** and **warning** mean:
        – A tornado **watch** means a tornado is possible in your area.
        – A tornado **warning** means a tornado has been sighted and may be headed towards you. Go to your safe area immediately.
    - Tornado **watches** and **warnings** are issued by the National Weather Service.

3. When a tornado **watch** is issued . . .
    - listen to local radio and TV stations for updates.
    - be alert to changes in weather conditions. Airborne debris or the sound of an approaching tornado should alert you. People who have heard one often say it sounds like a freight train.

4. When a tornado **warning** is issued . . .
    - If you are inside, go to the safe place you have selected to protect yourself from glass and other flying debris. The tornado may be approaching you.
    - If you are outside, hurry to the protection of a nearby sturdy building or lie flat in a ditch or low-lying area.

5. After the tornado passes . . .
    - watch out for fallen powerlines and stay out of damaged areas.
    - listen to the radio for information and instructions.
    - use a flashlight, if necessary, to inspect your home for damage.
    - do not use candles at any time, in case of gas leaks.

Giving Reasons

1. Listed below are the suggested materials for surviving a tornado. Next to each one give a reason why it is needed.

Materials	Reason Needed
first aid kit and essential medications	
canned food and can opener	
at least 4 gallons of water per person	
protective clothing, bedding, or sleeping bags	

Giving Reasons *(cont.)*

Name: _____

battery-powered radio, flashlight, and extra batteries	
special items for infant, elderly, or disabled family members	
written instructions on how to turn off electricity, gas, and water	

Researching

1. What other natural disasters are similar in destruction to tornadoes? You might need to look these up on the Internet or in a reference book. Here are some that cause great destruction. Complete the boxes for each disaster.

Type of Natural Event	Description of the Event *(what it is and how it causes damage)*
Tornado	
Volcanic eruption	
Tsunami	
Earthquake	
Cyclone	
Mudslide	
Floods	

Name: _____

Interpreting Graphs

1. The graphs below show the results of a survey completed by 40 boys and 40 girls about the different sports/hobbies they find interesting. Read the graphs and then answer the questions below.

Sports/Hobbies Girls Find Interesting

Sport/Hobby	Number of Girls Interested							
	5	10	15	20	25	30	35	40
football	▓	▓						
tennis	▓	▓	▓					
swimming	▓	▓	▓	▓	▓	▓	▓	▓
horseback riding	▓	▓	▓	▓	▓	▓		
karate	▓							
surfing	▓	▓	▓					
dancing	▓	▓	▓	▓	▓	▓	▓	
soccer	▓	▓	▓	▓	▓			
volleyball	▓	▓	▓	▓	▓	▓	▓	
computer games	▓	▓	▓	▓				

Sports/Hobbies Boys Find Interesting

Sport/Hobby	Number of Boys Interested							
	5	10	15	20	25	30	35	40
football	▓	▓	▓	▓	▓	▓	▓	
tennis	▓	▓	▓	▓	▓	▓		
swimming	▓	▓	▓	▓	▓	▓	▓	▓
horseback riding	▓							
karate	▓	▓	▓	▓	▓	▓		
surfing	▓	▓	▓	▓	▓	▓		
dancing	▓							
soccer	▓	▓	▓	▓	▓			
volleyball								
computer games	▓	▓	▓	▓	▓	▓	▓	▓

a. Which activity is liked by all boys and girls?

_____

b. How many more girls than boys like volleyball? _____

c. Which activities interest more than 30 girls?

_____

d. Which activities interest more than 30 boys?

_____

e. Is the statement "Boys and girls do not like the same activities" true or false? _____

f. Which activity do you think would cost the most to participate in? Why?

_____

_____

g. Which activities do girls like more than boys?

_____

h. Name a healthy activity most girls and boys are interested in.

_____

i. Which activities do you think would be the most risky?

_____

j. Can we tell from these graphs who participates in activities more—boys or girls? Give a reason for your answer.

_____

_____

Making a Survey

Here are the steps for making a survey:

1. Develop a survey question.
2. Prepare a response sheet.
3. Collect the responses from other students.
4. Group your responses according to the answers.
5. Tally the numbers for each answer.
6. Write your results (e.g., 30 out of 35 students ride a bike to school).

1. Survey 15 students in your class about their hobbies/interests. Choose one of the survey questions below.

- What is your favorite TV show?
- What food do you like the most?
- What sports do you like the most?
- What is your favorite book?
- What is your favorite movie?

Name: _____

Making a Survey (cont.)

2. Prepare a response sheet to collect your information. Write the question and then list the names of the students and their responses.

Question: _____

Student Name	Response

3. Group and tally your responses.

_____

_____

_____

_____

_____

_____

4. Write your results below.

_____

_____

_____

_____

Answer Key

Unit 1

Completing a Meaning Grid (page 8)

1. a. F—10, 20   e. T—9, 19   i. NE
   b. NE   f. F—13   j. T—3, 14
   c. T—10   g. F—16
   d. F—8   h. T—1

Providing Proof (page 9)

1. a. Chinese maps showing Australia in 600 B.C.E.–800 C.E.
   b. descriptions of Australian animals in Chinese writings
2. a. the discovery of a gold scarab, worshipped by the ancient Egyptians
   b. rock inscriptions, pyramids, and other Egyptian artifacts
3. a. They left artifacts behind.
   b. They mined for gold and other metals.
   c. The Japanese called Australia *Sei-tso*, meaning "the south land of pearls."
4. The sea routes for trading between the main settlements of the ancient world involved Australia.
5. They built towns and cities.

Words in Context (page 10)

1. a. enormous   h. gems
   b. civilizations   i. realized
   c. colonies, settlers   j. vessels
   d. Aboriginal Australians   k. inhabited
   e. worship   l. tongues
   f. dangerous   m. seaworthy
   g. relics   n. petrified
      o. pyramid

Matching (page 10)

1. a. Victoria   e. Myletus
   b. Chios   f. Daly River
   c. Gympie   g. China
   d. Japan   h. Mallos

Combining Sentences (page 11)

1. Answers will vary.

Unit 2

Letter-Writing Format (pages 14–15)

1. Reasons will vary for the following:
   a. yes   d. no   g. no
   b. yes   e. yes   h. no
   c. yes   f. yes   i. no

Unit 3

Words in Context (pages 18–19)

1. a. flying
   b. people involved
   c. height above sea level
   d. stopped
   e. secure and not changing
   f. move around and glide
   g. muscular strength
   h. something that stops you from doing a task
   i. rising hot air
   j. the way the land is formed as in valleys and hills
   k. in the air
   l. backup
   m. light wind
   n. the fewest (number)
   o. another (place or) choice

Supporting an Answer (pages 19–20)

1. Answers will vary.

Unit 4

Using the Dewey System (page 23)

1. a. General Works   i. Languages
   b. The Arts   j. History
   c. History   k. Natural Science
   d. Natural Science   l. Technology
   e. Natural Science   m. History
   f. Literature   n. Philosophy/Religion
   g. The Arts/Travel   o. Social Sciences
   h. Natural Science   p. History/Technology

Locating Books (page 23)

1. a. 600–699   i. 900–999
   b. 500–599   j. 600–699
   c. 200–299   k. 900–999
   d. 100–199   l. 700–799
   e. 300–399 and 900–999   m. 700–799
   f. 0–099   n. 600–699
   g. 900–999   o. 500–599
   h. 700–799   p. 400–499

Using Proofreading Skills (page 24)

1. Check answers for accuracy.

Extending Concepts (page 25)

1. a. books   g. websites   m. wheels
   b. pages   h. a list   n. a hose
   c. students   i. a string   o. fur
   d. words   j. an engine   p. legs
   e. information   k. a sink   q. streets
   f. shelves   l. a stem   r. a screen

ANSWER KEY

Classifying Analogies (pages 26–27)

1. vegetables
2. furniture
3. A table is always a piece of furniture; A piece of furniture is not always a table.
4. c   6. a   8. b   10. a   12. b
5. b   7. d   9. c   11. d   13. dogs
14. A poodle is always a dog; A dog is not always a poodle.
15. b   17. a   19. d   21. b   23. b
16. c   18. d   20. c   22. a

Unit 5

Paragraph Order (page 28)

5, 3, 7, 1, 6, 4, 2

Fact or Opinion (page 29)

1. a. fact   g. opinion   m. fact
   b. opinion   h. fact   n. opinion
   c. fact   i. fact   o. fact
   d. opinion   j. fact   p. opinion
   e. fact   k. opinion   q. opinion
   f. opinion   l. fact   r. opinion

Reading Critically (page 30)

Answers will vary.

Unit 7

Showing Understanding (pages 38–39)

1. a. T—1   e. F—3   i. T—5
   b. F—4   f. NE—6   j. T—2
   c. T—6   g. T—7
   d. F—5   h. NE—3, 6

Incorrect to Correct (page 39)

1. Check answers for accuracy.

Selecting the Main Idea (pages 40–41)

1. a. noun/pronoun: dinosaur; main idea: *T. rex* has become symbolic of most dinosaurs.
   b. noun/pronoun: atmosphere; main idea: The atmosphere makes looking into space difficult.
   c. noun/pronoun: electricity; main idea: Electricity affects all aspects of modern living.
   d. noun/pronoun: life (living beings); main idea: Now we believe that there are other living creatures in space.
   e. noun/pronoun: Crusoe/he; main idea: Crusoe was alone.
   f. noun/pronoun: giant/he; main idea: The man was extremely big.

Unit 8

Understanding Text Types (page 43)

1. a. recount   b. expository   c. procedure

Determining Text Types (page 44)

1. a. procedure   n. narrative
   b. report   o. procedure
   c. recount   p. expository
   d. narrative   q. recount
   e. explanation   r. procedure
   f. expository   s. report
   g. recount   t. expository
   h. narrative   u. recount
   i. procedure   v. narrative
   j. report   w. procedure
   k. recount   x. narrative
   l. explanation   y. procedure
   m. narrative   z. expository

Finding the Author's Purpose (page 45)

1. a. 6 b. 3 c. 2 d. 1 e. 4 f. 5 g. 3

Determining the Purpose (pages 46–47)

1. Answers will vary.

Unit 9

Using Context Clues (page 51)

2. a. coat/jacket   c. rhino
   b. angry   d. running/riding

Completing a Cloze Using Context Clues (page 52)

1. consists   8. baleen
2. tremendously   9. whale
3. ocean   10. seafood
4. Earth   11. ancient
5. krill   12. reasons
6. special   13. room
7. water   14. sea

Using Context to Get Meaning (page 53)

1. Answers will vary.

Unit 10

Reading Maps and Keys (pages 54–55)

1. a. south on Wellington Street, west on Hill Street, south on Hay Street
   b. south on St. George's Road
   c. north on Wellington Street, west on King Street
   d. east on William Street, south on St. George's Road, east on Pier Street
2. a. William Street, Barrack Street, Victoria Avenue
   b. City Mint (corner of Hill Street and Hay Street)
   c. Allan Green Observatory (corner of William Street and The Esplanade)
   d. Victoria Avenue, Queen Street

Answer Key (cont.)

3. a. by Old Mill Museum
   b. by Barrack Square and City Barracks
   c. by Governor's House

Interpreting a Map   (page 56)

1. a. T   f. F   k. F   p. F
   b. NE   g. T   l. T   q. T
   c. F   h. T   m. NE   r. T
   d. NE   i. T   n. T   s. NE
   e. F   j. T   o. T   t. T

Unit 11

Supporting Statements   (pages 59–60)

1. Answers will vary.

Completing an Event Grid   (page 60)

1. a. Father and Uncle—3
   b. Marco Polo—2
   c. Desert—6
   d. Desert—6
   e. Marco Polo, Father and Uncle—4
   f. Kublai Khan—1
   g. Desert—7
   h. Marco Polo, Father and Uncle—2
   i. Marco Polo, Father and Uncle—2
   j. Marco Polo—2
   k. Marco Polo—1
   l. Kublai Khan—1
   m. Desert—8
   n. Marco Polo—1

Thinking Critically   (page 61)

1. Answers will vary.

Associating Word Meanings   (page 62)

1. Suggested answers:
   a. barren, harsh, sand
   b. grass, water, plants, camp
   c. strong, herbivore, hump
   d. ruler, powerful, ruthless, warrior
   e. horsemen, fierce, yurts, tribal
   f. merchants, sea, trade
   g. Persia, Armenia, Venice
   h. eerie, strange, imagined
   i. saddle, strong, tame
   j. crew, mast, sail, cargo
   k. goods, money, merchants, banks
   l. tent, large, shelter, felt
   m. horse, ship, plane, road
   n. forests, lakes, rocks, slopes, snow
   o. water, ships, trade, storms

Wrong to Right   (page 62)

1. a. strange
   b. young
   c. good
   d. well-traveled/well-established

Unit 12

Matching Terms and Definitions   (page 63)

1. compass—k   jackhammer—i
   cherry picker—d   periscope—h
   electric drill—l   satellite—o
   vault—a   circular saw—p
   generator—n   spark plug—j
   extension ladder—e   jet ski—m
   electric shovel—c   scuba tanks—f
   monorail—b   Mars Rover—g

Interpreting Pictures   (page 64)

1. a. T   e. F   i. PT or T
   b. F   f. F   j. NE
   c. NE   g. NE   k. PT
   d. PT   h. PF   l. PF

Expanding Sentences   (page 67)

1. Answers will vary.

Understanding Explanatory Texts   (pages 68–69)

1. Answers will vary.

Giving Reasons   (pages 70–71)

1. Answers will vary.

Researching   (page 71)

1. Answers will vary.

Unit 13

Interpreting Graphs   (pages 72–73)

1. a. swimming
   b. 35
   c. swimming, dancing, volleyball
   d. tennis, swimming, surfing, computer games
   e. False; many girls and boys like the same activities.
   f. Answers will vary.
   g. horseback riding, dancing, volleyball
   h. swimming
   i. Answers will vary.
   j. Girls—220, boys—235; in this graph, the boys participated more, but both are involved.

Meeting Standards

Each activity meets one or more of the following Common Core State Standards (© Copyright 2010. National Governors Association Center for Best Practices and Council of Chief State School Officers. All rights reserved.). For more information about the Common Core State Standards, go to *http://www.corestandards.org/* or *http://www.teachercreated.com/standards*.

Grade 7

Reading: Literature	Page
Key Ideas and Details	
ELA.RL.7.1: Cite several pieces of textual evidence to support analysis of what the text says explicitly as well as inferences drawn from the text.	30, 46–47
ELA.RL.7.2: Determine a theme or central idea of a text and analyze its development over the course of the text; provide an objective summary of the text.	46–48
Craft and Structure	
ELA.RL.7.4: Determine the meaning of words and phrases as they are used in a text, including figurative and connotative meanings; analyze the impact of rhymes and other repetitions of sounds (e.g., alliteration) on a specific verse or stanza of a poem or section of a story or drama.	12–13, 30, 46–48
ELA.RL.7.5: Analyze how a drama's or poem's form or structure (e.g., soliloquy, sonnet) contributes to its meaning.	47–48
Range of Reading and Level of Text Complexity	
ELA.RL.7.10: By the end of the year, read and comprehend literature, including stories, dramas, and poems, in the grades 6–8 text complexity band proficiently, with scaffolding as needed at the high end of the range.	12–13, 30, 46–48

Reading: Informational Text	Page
Key Ideas and Details	
ELA.RI.7.1: Cite several pieces of textual evidence to support analysis of what the text says explicitly as well as inferences drawn from the text.	5–8, 14–17, 19–20, 38–39, 42, 54–56, 58–60, 72–73
ELA.RI.7.2: Determine two or more central ideas in a text and analyze their development over the course of the text; provide an objective summary of the text.	8–9, 28, 38–39, 42, 65–71
ELA.RI.7.3: Analyze the interactions between individuals, events, and ideas in a text (e.g., how ideas influence individuals or events, or how individuals influence ideas or events).	5–8, 19–20, 29, 58–60, 65–67, 69–70, 73–74
Craft and Structure	
ELA.RI.7.4: Determine the meaning of words and phrases as they are used in a text, including figurative, connotative, and technical meanings; analyze the impact of a specific word choice on meaning and tone.	5–7, 14–17, 19–20, 28, 38–41, 50–52, 54–55, 60, 67–69, 71–73
ELA.RI.7.6: Determine an author's point of view or purpose in a text and analyze how the author distinguishes his or her position from that of others.	32–33, 45
Integration of Knowledge and Ideas	
ELA.RI.7.8: Trace and evaluate the argument and specific claims in a text, assessing whether the reasoning is sound and the evidence is relevant and sufficient to support the claims.	19–20, 29, 32–33, 59–60
Range of Reading and Level of Text Complexity	
ELA.RI.7.10: By the end of the year, read and comprehend literary nonfiction in the grades 6–8 text complexity band proficiently, with scaffolding as needed at the high end of the range.	5–7, 16–17, 22–23, 28, 32–33, 38, 40–41, 43–45, 52, 54–56, 58–59, 64, 65–70, 72–73

Writing	Page
Text Types and Purposes	
ELA.W.7.1: Write arguments to support claims with clear reasons and relevant evidence.	19–21, 33–37, 59–60
ELA.W.7.2: Write informative/explanatory texts to examine a topic and convey ideas, concepts, and information through the selection, organization, and analysis of relevant content.	5–9, 11–15, 19–21, 31, 42, 54–55, 57, 67, 72–74
ELA.W.7.3: Write narratives to develop real or imagined experiences or events using effective technique, relevant descriptive details, and well-structured event sequences.	12–13, 21, 31, 48–49
Production and Distribution of Writing	
ELA.W.7.4: Produce clear and coherent writing in which the development, organization, and style are appropriate to task, purpose, and audience. (Grade-specific expectations for writing types are defined in standards 1–3 above.)	5–8, 11–13, 21, 31, 48–49, 57, 73–74
ELA.W.7.5: With some guidance and support from peers and adults, develop and strengthen writing as needed by planning, revising, editing, rewriting, or trying a new approach, focusing on how well purpose and audience have been addressed.	33–37

Meeting Standards *(cont.)*

Writing *(cont.)*	Page
Research to Build and Present Knowledge	
ELA.W.7.8: Gather relevant information from multiple print and digital sources, using search terms effectively; assess the credibility and accuracy of each source; and quote or paraphrase the data and conclusions of others while avoiding plagiarism and following a standard format for citation.	71
ELA.W.7.9: Draw evidence from literary or informational texts to support analysis, reflection, and research.	5–9, 19–20, 65–67, 71–74
Range of Writing	
ELA.W.7.10: Write routinely over extended time frames (time for research, reflection, and revision) and shorter time frames (a single sitting or a day or two) for a range of discipline-specific tasks, purposes, and audiences.	5–9, 12–15, 19–21, 31, 33–37, 39, 42, 48–50, 54–55, 57, 59–60, 67, 70–74

Language	Page
Conventions of Standard English	
ELA.L.7.1: Demonstrate command of the conventions of standard English grammar and usage when writing or speaking.	9, 12–13, 19–21, 31, 33–37, 48–50, 67
ELA.L.7.2: Demonstrate command of the conventions of standard English capitalization, punctuation, and spelling when writing.	9, 12–13, 19–21, 24, 31, 33–37, 48–50, 59–60, 67
Knowledge of Language	
ELA.L.7.3: Use knowledge of language and its conventions when writing, speaking, reading, or listening.	9, 12–13, 19–21, 24, 31, 33–37, 40–41, 43–44, 48–50, 52, 59–61, 63, 67–71
Vocabulary Acquisition and Use	
ELA.L.7.4: Determine or clarify the meaning of unknown and multiple-meaning words and phrases based on grade 7 reading and content, choosing flexibly from a range of strategies.	all activities
ELA.L.7.5: Demonstrate understanding of figurative language, word relationships, and nuances in word meanings.	10, 18–19, 25–27, 50–51, 53, 62
ELA.L.7.6: Acquire and use accurately grade-appropriate general academic and domain-specific words and phrases; gather vocabulary knowledge when considering a word or phrase important to comprehension or expression.	10, 18–19, 22–27, 40–41, 43–44, 46–55, 60, 63, 67, 71–74

Grade 8

Reading: Literature	Page
Key Ideas and Details	
ELA.RL.8.1: Cite the textual evidence that most strongly supports an analysis of what the text says explicitly as well as inferences drawn from the text.	30, 46–47
ELA.RL.8.2: Determine a theme or central idea of a text and analyze its development over the course of the text, including its relationship to the characters, setting, and plot; provide an objective summary of the text.	46–48
Craft and Structure	
ELA.RL.8.4: Determine the meaning of words and phrases as they are used in a text, including figurative and connotative meanings; analyze the impact of specific word choices on meaning and tone, including analogies or allusions to other texts.	12–13, 30, 46–48
ELA.RL.8.5: Compare and contrast the structure of two or more texts and analyze how the differing structure of each text contributes to its meaning and style.	47–48
Range of Reading and Level of Text Complexity	
ELA.RL.8.10: By the end of the year, read and comprehend literature, including stories, dramas, and poems, at the high end of grades 6–8 text complexity band independently and proficiently.	12–13, 30, 46–48

Reading: Informational Text	Page
Key Ideas and Details	
ELA.RI.8.1: Cite the textual evidence that most strongly supports an analysis of what the text says explicitly as well as inferences drawn from the text.	5–8, 14–17, 19–20, 38–39, 42, 54–56, 58–60, 72–73
ELA.RI.8.2: Determine a central idea of a text and analyze its development over the course of the text, including its relationship to supporting ideas; provide an objective summary of the text.	8–9, 28, 38–39, 42, 65–71
ELA.RI.8.3: Analyze how a text makes connections among and distinctions between individuals, ideas, or events (e.g., through comparisons, analogies, or categories).	5–8, 19–20, 26–27, 29, 58–60, 65–67, 69–70, 73–74

Reading: Informational Text (cont.)	Page
Craft and Structure	
ELA.RI.8.4: Determine the meaning of words and phrases as they are used in a text, including figurative, connotative, and technical meanings; analyze the impact of specific word choices on meaning and tone, including analogies or allusions to other texts.	5–7, 14–17, 19–20, 28, 38–41, 50–52, 54–55, 60, 67–69, 71–73
ELA.RI.8.5: Analyze in detail the structure of a specific paragraph in a text, including the role of particular sentences in developing and refining a key concept.	8–9, 59–60
ELA.RI.8.6: Determine an author's point of view or purpose in a text and analyze how the author acknowledges and responds to conflicting evidence or viewpoints.	32–33, 45
Integration of Knowledge and Ideas	
ELA.RI.8.8: Delineate and evaluate the argument and specific claims in a text, assessing whether the reasoning is sound and the evidence is relevant and sufficient; recognize when irrelevant evidence is introduced.	19–20, 29, 32–33, 59–60
Range of Reading and Level of Text Complexity	
ELA.RI.8.10: By the end of the year, read and comprehend literary nonfiction at the high end of the grades 6–8 text complexity band independently and proficiently.	5–7, 16–17, 22–23, 28, 32–33, 38, 40–41, 43–45, 52, 54–56, 58–59, 64–70, 72–73

Writing	Page
Text Types and Purposes	
ELA.W.8.1: Write arguments to support claims with clear reasons and relevant evidence.	19–21, 33–37, 59–60
ELA.W.8.2: Write informative/explanatory texts to examine a topic and convey ideas, concepts, and information through the selection, organization, and analysis of relevant content.	5–9, 11–15, 19–21, 31, 42, 54–55, 57, 67, 72–74
ELA.W.8.3: Write narratives to develop real or imagined experiences or events using effective technique, relevant descriptive details, and well-structured event sequences.	12–13, 21, 31, 48–49
Production and Distribution of Writing	
ELA.W.8.4: Produce clear and coherent writing in which the development, organization, and style are appropriate to task, purpose, and audience. (Grade-specific expectations for writing types are defined in standards 1–3 above.)	5–8, 11–13, 21, 31, 48–49, 57, 73–74
ELA.W.8.5: With some guidance and support from peers and adults, develop and strengthen writing as needed by planning, revising, editing, rewriting, or trying a new approach, focusing on how well purpose and audience have been addressed.	33–37
Research to Build and Present Knowledge	
ELA.W.8.8: Gather relevant information from multiple print and digital sources, using search terms effectively; assess the credibility and accuracy of each source; and quote or paraphrase the data and conclusions of others while avoiding plagiarism and following a standard format for citation.	71
ELA.W.8.9: Draw evidence from literary or informational texts to support analysis, reflection, and research.	5–9, 19–20, 65–67, 71–74
Range of Writing	
ELA.W.8.10: Write routinely over extended time frames (time for research, reflection, and revision) and shorter time frames (a single sitting or a day or two).	5–9, 12–15, 19–21, 31, 33–37, 39, 42, 48–50, 54–55, 57, 59–60, 67, 70–74

Language	Page
Conventions of Standard English	
ELA.L.8.1: Demonstrate command of the conventions of standard English grammar and usage when writing or speaking.	9, 12–13, 19–21, 31, 33–37, 48–50, 67
ELA.L.8.2: Demonstrate command of the conventions of standard English capitalization, punctuation, and spelling when writing.	9, 12–13, 19–21, 24, 31, 33–37, 48–50, 59–60, 67
Knowledge of Language	
ELA.L.8.3: Use knowledge of language and its conventions when writing, speaking, reading, or listening.	9, 12–13, 19–21, 24, 31, 33–37, 40–41, 43–44, 48–50, 52, 59–61, 63, 67–71
Vocabulary Acquisition and Use	
ELA.L.8.4: Determine or clarify the meaning of unknown and multiple-meaning words and phrases based on grade 8 reading and content, choosing flexibly from a range of strategies.	all activities
ELA.L.8.5: Demonstrate understanding of figurative language, word relationships, and nuances in word meanings.	10, 18–19, 25–27, 50–51, 53, 62
ELA.L.8.6: Acquire and use accurately grade-appropriate general academic and domain-specific words and phrases; gather vocabulary knowledge when considering a word or phrase important to comprehension or expression.	10, 18–19, 22–27, 40–41, 43–44, 46–55, 60, 63, 67, 71–74